The Dimensions of Writing

G000147758

The Dimensions of Writing

Ann Kinmont
Principal Lecturer,
King Alfred's College, Winchester

David Fulton Publishers
London

David Fulton Publishers Ltd
2 Barbon Close, London WC1N 3JX

First published in Great Britain by
David Fulton Publishers 1990

British Library Cataloguing in Publication Data

Kinmont, Ann
    The dimensions of writing.
    1. Primary schools. Curriculum subjects: Writing skills.
    Teaching
    I. Title
    372.623044

    ISBN 1-85346-130-X

Typeset by Chapterhouse, Formby
Printed in Great Britain by BPCC Wheatons Ltd, Exeter

Contents

Foreword

The development of children's writing competence challenges both teacher and researcher with a set of frustrating mysteries. On the one hand we know that many children become more skilled in the craft the longer they remain in school. On the other hand we cannot either describe or explain the progress very well; neither can we explain which activities will promote or retard development.

At present then we suffer from a paradox. We can point to better or worse pieces of writing. It is not difficult to demonstrate consensus about such comparisons if we create large enough differences. However, as soon as we begin to apply any analytic schemes to diagnose the bases of our evaluations, they fail to capture the quality of the differences. How are we to encourage children to evaluate and improve their writing if we cannot describe what is better in linguistic terms? How are they to develop their own evaluative criteria if we can not specify these?

Yet somehow the developments occur. Across time and space, children improve. While we cannot describe or explain, we can create conditions that work. What is more encouraging is that we are probably getting much better than we were at enabling children to become better writers.

As Ann Kinmont illustrates, it is only in the last few years that serious attention has been given to the psychological processes involved in writing. It is only in recent years that more general theories of the intellectual, motivational and emotional development of children have been used to provide a framework for expectation and practice. It is only in recent years that we have begun to escape from two uncomfortable and unproductive forms of a misconstrued dilemma.

The obsession with the teaching and marking of punctuation, spelling, vocabulary and what aspired to be 'grammar' was driven in part by the need to make objective assessments of children's work and to demonstrate that schools were maintaining standards. Other qualities of writing were deemed to be too subjective to permit marking.

The sterility of this narrow vision was replaced by notions about the encouragement of creativity which rushed us to another equally narrow perspective. With little knowledge of the units and structures available to be creative with, children were required to express themselves freely.

Ann Kinmont's text is a timely attempt at reconciliation and balance. She demonstrates the varieties of writing required of us and points to the differing activities appropriate for learning these. We need to write out shopping lists as well as our variants of odes to nightingales. The eclecticism acts to moderate the exaggeration of the wilder propagandists. The linkage between theory and classroom practice begins to create the dialogue which will eventually lead to progress in our own understanding.

In the meantime Ann Kinmont offers us an accurate and clearly articulated review of the state of the art, a portrait of classroom possibilities, and an analysis of the opportunities and dangers in evaluation.

Peter Robinson
March 1990

INTRODUCTION

An Overview of Writing Research

Observational studies indicate that writing is one of the main features of children's primary school experience, one estimate suggesting that 30% of junior school pupils' time is taken up in writing activity (Galton *et al*, 1980, p. 81). However, despite a general increase in research studies into language development over the past decade, writing has tended to receive less attention than, for example, reading. The Bullock Report (DES, 1975) reflects this tendency, giving distinctly more space to reading and associated activities than to writing.

There are, of course, books devoted to the latter – many adopt a narrow perspective and are generally inconclusive if a consideration of the whole range of issues about writing is required. Others consider the place of writing within the wider context of literacy, for example, Smith (1982) and Hall (1987). Some describe broad patterns of classroom practice as for instance, in the HMI reports on primary and first schools, (DES, 1978, 1982a) and in the Oracle project, (Galton *et al*, 1980) but do not attempt a critical analysis. Graves (1983) in particular, has focused on what teachers and pupils actually do in writing sessions, while Bereiter (1980) puts an emphasis on both process and product. Such descriptions of the writing process as do exist are mostly related to the secondary school age range (e.g. Burgess *et al*, 1973; Britton *et al*, 1975; Martin *et al*, 1976). While some studies have focused on 'creative writing' in the junior school years (Maybury, 1967; Marshall, 1974) others have adopted a wider framework, but remain descriptive rather than analytical (Rosen and Rosen, 1973; Hutchcroft *et al*, 1981). Arguably there is more substance in Harpin's (1976) study, which considered a range of linguistic features to determine whether or not they provided a measure of maturation in writing. This project reflected the approach of an earlier researcher, La Brant (1933), whose method of analysis was later refined by Hunt (1965).

Recent studies reflect the current interest in promoting techniques for effective intervention in the writing process – work which has been influential in guiding the research of the National Writing Project. The general findings of these studies indicate what to most primary school teachers is immediately obvious – that as children of average and above-average ability mature as writers they produce writing of increasing length, employing longer and more complex sentences and showing greater variety and competency in syntactic structure.

All this information is valuable and helpful in providing the means for objective assessment of children's writing. It does not, however, isolate areas of difficulty or differentiate between types of writing. Nor does it identify distinct stages of development or necessarily indicate strategies upon which the promotion of more effective writing may be based. Nevertheless, there are areas in which, in recent years, there has been growth in understanding of writing as a process. Although studies have taken a range of theoretical perspectives, there is now increasing evidence of the relationship between speech and writing; greater knowledge of the nature and internal organisation of written texts; and, crucially, some insight into the complexities of the writing process.

Wilkinson (1980, 1986) and Beard (1984) have specifically addressed the issue of development in writing and sought to more closely inform classroom practice. Much still remains speculative about the nature of the writing process, but there is now clear evidence of certain sequential features in children's writing which occur with maturation, and which could provide the basis of a development model.

Perhaps one of the reasons for the dearth of conclusive information on writing is the difficulty researchers necessarily face in distinguishing between writing activity and all other language activities across the curriculum. 'Language' tasks, as such, will be associated with history, geography, science, religious studies and environmental studies, whether or not embraced under the 'topic work' umbrella; some writing will even be included in areas of mathematics. The examination of language in the curriculum also has to take account of the many pedagogic practices based consciously or unconsciously on the notion that pupils will do most of their learning through language, and there is a commonly held assumption that a significant part of the teacher's work is to develop pupils' language.

There are those teachers who believe that development will occur naturally and simply as a result of maturation; others see a definite need for 'fostering' techniques. Inevitably teachers will differ in the emphasis put on different aspects, and there are many areas in which there will not always be agreement. The 'creative writing' movement of the 1960s has tended, for example, to perpetuate a distinction – especially in primary schools – between 'creative writing' and all other kinds of written work. This in turn has led to uncertainty as to how different types of writing should be classified and to some confusion in terminology in relation to the forms and functions of written language. But as Beard reminds us:

> Writing is one of the four modes of the system of human communication that we call language. It is a capacity which, together with talking, listening and reading, sets people clearly apart from other creatures of the earth on the evolutionary scale.
>
> (Beard, 1984, p. 20)

It is therefore not easy to isolate writing from other mutually-facilitating activities, nor to observe clear distinctions between complex, interdependent processes.

Thus attempts to come to terms with the problem have, in the main, concentrated on models of language development in general and have been related to prevailing theories of teaching and learning. Though he did not produce a conclusive theory, Moffett in his *Teaching the Universe of Discourse*, went some way towards an explanation:

> The most sensible strategy for determining a proper learning order in English, it seems to me, is to look for the main lines of child development, and to assimilate to them, when fitting, the various formulations that scholars make about language and literature.
>
> (Moffett, 1968, p. 14)

Moffett sees growth as predominantly related to cognition, with a natural (though not obvious) correlation between thought and language.

Historically, it is possible to identify three major models. The skills model focuses on mechanics and techniques of expression rather than on the quality of what is expressed. Within an examination system it allows for a certain objectivity in marking and assessment, perhaps at the expense of more individual and subjective features. Wilkinson (1980) refers to the 'cultural heritage' model which introduces a liberal element to the skills model, and which has sustained a polarity between language and literacy in the curriculum. This model relates to the transmission of culture, and could be considered inadequate in that it ignores the pupils' own creative abilities and contributions. Probably the most influential interpretation of the model was presented in the HMSO Report: *The Teaching of English in England* (1923).

Contemporary models spring from the child-centred emphasis in education which has dominated recent decades, and they are essentially concerned with personal growth. Interest focuses on the development of the individual and the means by which experiences are defined and understood. In this personal growth model, priority is given to self-expression and to the interpretation and articulation of ideas. The 'context' model attempts a fusion of the heritage and personal models, its proponents claiming that the social background of the individual cannot be ignored in the teaching and learning of language. In a paper giving evidence to the Bullock Committee in 1973, the National Association for the Teaching of English argue:

> Aspects of language itself, speaking, listening, writing and reading, must be seen in context with one another. The neglect of oracy and the frequent isolated treatment of reading are too notorious to need further comment at this point.
>
> (NATE, 1969, para. 1.3.2.)

The work of James Britton (1975) for the Schools Council Research Project has exerted considerable influence on current thinking. His model, which owes its origins to Moffett amongst others, is, in part, an attempt to acount for the development of two differentiated forms of writing – transactional (persuasive and informative) writing, and poetic (creative) writing. The aim of the project

> ... was to undertake a developmental study of the process by which the written language of young children becomes differentiated, during the years eleven to eighteen, into kinds of written discourse appropriate to different purposes.
>
> (Britton *et al*, 1975, p. 50).

Britton's model offers three main functions set on a continuum in which the central category is the 'expressive' one – a form of writing that is informal, intimate and unstructured, verbalising the inner consciousness. The continuum extends to include poetic language in which the writer can focus on the forms and patterns of language itself, creating a 'work of art'; and to transactional language, which is the language of information such as recording, reporting and letter-writing. Two roles are thus distinguished for the writer – that of the spectator in poetic language, and the participant in transactional writing. Both roles, Britton argues, depend on cognition in the representation of reality and in reflections upon it.

Although his research was related specifically to the development of writing abilities in secondary age pupils, the features he describes do have relevance in relation to younger pupils, and his work has provided a theoretical framework for other research. It was used, for example, as the basis for the sections on writing in the Bullock Report (DES, 1975). In particular his model allows for an examination of the development of thought as it shows itself in written language. But it cannot be regarded as a comprehensive theory in that it is not concerned with stylistic growth in writing, nor does it encompass social, emotional or moral aspects of development.

Indeed, it has become increasingly obvious that to substantiate such models, a theory of the development of the human personality is essential. As Wilkinson states:

> There are clear differences between the language of, say, a six year old and a sixteen year old. Development takes place, but it does not take place obviously.
> (Wilkinson *et al*, in Kroll and Wells, 1983, p. 43)

Clearly there are activities which teachers undertake in relation to writing which could possibly be more effective if they were closely informed by some understanding of the stages through which children pass in their development as writers. An awareness for example, of the varying demands made by different kinds of writing might enable the setting of tasks more appropriate to children's ages and abilities. It could also inform teachers' responses to the marking and correction of written products, highlighting not only errors but also their causes, and guide towards positive remedial action. Similarly, in the assessment of writing which involves making judgements, the sharper the criteria, the more reliable those judgements are likely to be.

A developmental perspective would emphasise that not all criteria need be linguistic. Obviouly, the range and appropriateness of vocabulary, general structure and cohesion are important factors, but a realistic assessment must also take account of elements such as as liveliness, humour, imagination, neatness and so on – all aspects of personality. There is therefore a sense in which it is impossible to isolate writing development from all other aspects of language growth. Individual writing quality will be significantly enhanced by inputs from oral language, from reading and comprehension; the gradual accumulation of information and the building up of experiences, will be reflected in all these developing competencies. They provide easily observable evidence of growth in understanding and awareness and indicate the range and quality of the cognitive resources being drawn on.

It is against this background that the Crediton Language Development Project emerged, from work being undertaken at Exeter University Language in Education Centre. Its findings were initially published in 1980 (Wilkinson *et al.*) and subsequently developed. The researchers offer a developmental perspective which grew out of a dissatisfaction with the existing criteria of judgements used for children's writing, which have a tendency to emphasise the learning of the component skills of writing, which can be readily marked. Instead of using selective linguistic criteria they argue for judgements to be based on a view of the development of the individual as a 'communicating being'. This, it is believed, offers possibilities for the exploration of both the complexity of written work and the elements in the relationship between writer, writing and reader. For the project, four models of development were devised – stylistic, cognitive, affective and moral, and based on an interaction between perceptions of written materials, teachers' judgements and theoretical consider-ations. Their conclusions suggest that there are strong grounds for believing that the nature of the writing task, and the context for writing, exert a considerable influence on the outcomes.

The approach adopted by Bereiter (1980) focuses on the process, the product and the reader and he comes close to an integration of Wilkinson's cognitive and affective models. He identifies five basic stages in writing development, and implies that making one stage automatic greatly facilitates progress to the next stage. But he believes that pupils do not always get sufficient practice in the control and mastery of stylistic conventions, and therefore lose valuable oppor-tunities to fully extend writing competence. Traditional classroom practices tend to act as a constraint and products become more important than the process in what Frank Smith (1982) calls 'only one-chance writing'.

Helping children to devise strategies and self-cueing techniques for developing writing has been a focus of the research of Bereiter and Scardamalia (1982), particularly in relation to the composing process. Their work suggests that there are ways in which teachers can constructively intervene in the writing process to support pupils, by means of what they term 'facilitative procedures.'

Building on the notion of intervention while children are actually writing, Donald Graves (1983) proposed the setting up of a pupil/teacher 'conference'. His strategies are based on writing as a joint venture, in which teachers create classroom practices and procedures which encourage and facilitate writing. Teachers are encouraged to engage in writing themselves, acting as a model for the pupils.

His recommendations have been taken up and developed in the School Curriculum Development Committee's National Writing Project. This three year project, running from 1985 to 1987, focused on writers between five and sixteen years of age. Its scope was the whole curriculum, and the range of purposes for writing which were identified in all subjects, topics and activities. The participating teachers, for this was an essentially school-based programme, took a view of writing as 'an integral part of a learning process, not simply proof that the learning had taken place'. In drawing directly on the work of teachers and children in schools, it has made an important contribution both in directing classroom practice more purposefully and in raising teacher expectations. Publication of the general and specific conclusions, and of evidence of good practice in writing development, together with an acknowledgement of the substance of the research in the Cox Report (1988) has ensured that current thinking will be more widely disseminated in schools.

Although much still remains speculative about the nature of the writing process, there is increasing evidence for the existence of what Beard (1984) terms, 'predictable patterns of linguistic development in children's writing'. It becomes much easier to clarify the purposes for writing where there is some understanding of the stage of development through which a child is passing. But writing serves a number of purposes; there is the utilitarian one – as a vehicle for expressing knowledge and for exploring the curriculum. It also has a more personal function; writing confirms and articulates thoughts and focuses attention on language as a medium for organising experience. It may even, as Smith asserts, act as a catalyst in promoting and extending thought:

Writing is not simply a matter of putting down on paper

8

ideas that we already have in our heads. Many ideas would not exist if they were not created on paper.

(Smith, 1983, p. 79)

The potential for cognitive growth that writing engenders, has been well documented by Wilkinson (1980) and Bereiter (1980) in particular, and their research indicates the extent to which writing reflects individual personality and the process of maturation. What does seem to emerge is the fact that an individual construction of meaning is crucial to confidence and performance in writing. Their work offers a theoretical justification for a study of the nature of thought, of the feeling, of the moral stance, as well as the style evident in children's writing.

There are clear benefits to be gained from the systematic analysis of actual scripts but there are now equally clear indications that the context in which writing takes place, the role the teacher adopts in relation to it, the purpose of the writing and the audience for whom it is intended, are all important factors in the undertaking, and will have a significant bearing on the finished product. What children write and the manner in which it is written, gives us crucial information about them, and Graves (1983) in particular, in recommending that teachers write with their pupils, is encouraging a clearer perception of the difficulties children encounter. A better understanding of the process of writing could guide towards actual improvement.

If children are to gain confidence in themselves as writers, and to master the complex process of writing, they need every possible opportunity to write continuously in a variety of ways and for a range of purposes. The intention is that writing should become a powerful tool for understanding, interpreting, reflecting and translating the child's engagement with and experience of the world. This, Smith (1982) has argued, will occur where children learn to write as naturally as they learn to talk – 'without being aware that they are doing so, in the course of doing other things'. Writing is a natural activity, though not, as Peel has indicated:

. . . as easy and immediate as talking or listening nor such obvious fun as play but still a natural means of self-expression. But, first, children must have a reason for writing. They must have something that they are eager to write about, that is alive for them, actually, or in their minds, as they write, that touches their experience'.

(Peel, 1967, p. 137)

Much of the responsibility for sustaining excitement and involvement in writing lies with the teacher, who has to recognise and respond to writing as both a communicative and a psychological process. The National Curriculum Report (*English for Ages 5 to 16*, 1989) advises that 'structured and sensitive teaching is . . . essential if children's development as writers is to thrive'. It is particularly important that children learn what to say and how to say it, before notions of correctness and convention are imposed upon their efforts in writing.

Good primary teachers pay attention to the process of writing, developed from knowledge and understanding of the practice of experienced writers (including themselves); they are then able to provide classroom practices which allow children to behave like real writers.

(DES, 1989, 3, 3.13)

CHAPTER 1

The Classroom Context

The primary classroom aspires to being a natural setting for children's learning. To this end, in post-Plowden years, its character has become increasingly informal, moving away from class-based teaching towards individualised learning. At the most superficial level this informality is evident in the arrangement of groups of children at tables, in the carpeted and cushioned reading corners, in the bright, eye-catching displays, in the freedom of movement that is encouraged and tolerated and in the lively bustle and chatter of the pupils.

Closer inspection reveals that the teacher interacts with individual children, with groups of children, and occasionally with the whole class. A survey of the tasks on which children are engaged, will indicate that a number of activities are in progress simultaneously, and that children may well move from one task to another during a session, with minimal teacher direction. There is an element of self-sufficiency in operation and the children are exerting a considerable freedom of choice in what to do, when to do it and how to do it. At times they may appear to opt to do very little, but for the most part they will, to a greater or lesser degree, be actively engaged in the task in hand.

Tradition and practice

This shift in emphasis has been well-documented, both in general description and through the systematic study of pupils and teachers at work. What has emerged is that although classrooms exhibit marked differences, there are characteristic features common to all primary classrooms. These occur principally at the level of the curriculum, that is, the actual learning experiences which are provided. In this respect, observers (Galton, Simon and Croll, 1980) have noted that tradition still exerts a strong influence, and long-standing practices and routines in task allocation and demand are still much in evidence. The emphasis on literacy and numeracy continues, while other curricular areas are subsumed under the general heading of topic or project work.

In line with the organisational changes, and related to prevailing educational psychology, teachers have adopted what Bennett, Desforges, Cockburn and Wilkinson (1984) term, a 'philosophy of individualisation', a concern for the social, emotional and physical well-being of each child within the educational context. The 'child-centred' approach, as it is described, assumes that teachers are providing a curriculum individually tailored to meet all the child's developmental needs. In practice, this is a difficult approach to operate successfully, and it has given rise to the integrated day, topic work, family grouping, workcards and rotating activities, for example, as strategies for teaching. The problems of matching work for children of differing abilities and attainments, within an informal structure, have been highlighted in the H.M.I. survey of 1978, and the demands on teachers' time and energies are great.

As a consequence, the teaching and learning situation which currently prevails in primary schools requires that the teacher be highly organised and efficient. A majority of teachers, if only to preserve their sanity, strive to achieve a balance between informal and formal teaching and methodology; relatively few operate at the extremes.

Teaching and learning

In order to meet the challenge, teachers have turned increasingly to group-based activity as a basis for classroom management. This was the economy recommended by the Plowden Report (1967), as a way to counter the then perceived emphasis on class instruction. Group work was seen to have both a pedagogic role and also to fulfil a social function, with particular benefits for the shy or timid child; benefits which have been reiterated by H.M.I. (in D.E.S., 1982). The collaborative nature of group work, its potential for discussion and enquiry and for independent learning, is being successfully exploited in primary classrooms, and some pupils do experience a richness and breadth of curricular activity. But for a significant number of pupils, as Boydell (1975) and Bennett, Desforges, Cockburn and Wilkinson (1984) have reported, group work is less than satisfying, bringing a decline in pupil involvement and performance through delay, inter-ruption and social distraction.

'Observational research and classroom evaluation'

The ORACLE (Observational Research and Classroom Evaluation) research of the early 1980s, the first large-scale observational study of primary classrooms, focused on patterns of activity and instruction, on teaching styles and on aspects of classroom organisation. Their objective was to identify and analyse the effectiveness of different teaching styles. But while they conclude that many teachers have absorbed the Plowden philosophy, they also observe that a number have failed to effectively translate theory into practice.

The published findings, Galton and Simon (1980), present a profile of the successful teacher as one who sustains above-average levels of interaction with pupils; ensures the smooth running of classroom routines; involves the children in high level statements and questioning; gives clear directions and instructions and encourages children to adopt their own strategies for solving problems.

This survey, and subsequent research such as that of Bennett, Desforges, Cockburn and Wilkinson (1984), for example, reminds us of the teacher's central role in the classroom and confirms that the teacher is an important determinant of pupil progress. The classroom is, as every teacher is aware, a complex organisation in which many elements, some conflicting, some complementary, combine to create the circumstances for teaching and learning. The teacher dictates the manner and style of this encounter, bringing together a personal philosophy and pedagogy and pupils' experience and expectations, within the school's ideology and practice. As Shipman (1979) has remarked, this can be a matter of accommodation and compromise and the 'goodness of fit is often marginal'.

The essential link between pupils and teacher is the curriculum, what it comprises, how it is interpreted, the tasks that are set and the nature of classroom activity. The degree to which it actively promotes learning and the level of intellectual challenge it offers will have a significant effect on pupils' responses, their concentration and effort and ultimately on the quality of their learning experience. The dynamic classroom is one which does not simply reinforce existing knowledge and skills but encourages pupils to develop and extend their capabilities and competencies.

Classroom writing

The classroom context has important consequences for all teaching and learning, but especially so in respect of writing. It is the means by which the curriculum is translated – it offers evidence that teaching has taken place; it is a mechanism of control, occupying and engaging pupils' concentration; it indicates effort and commitment to teachers, parents and other children and therefore, also serves an evaluative function.

As a consequence, quantity, neatness and accuracy become the chief objectives and the importance of writing inevitably lies in products. For a majority of children, the classroom is the crucial setting in which writing is learned and practised and it is for this reason that we have to take account of what Beard describes as the

> dynamic relationship between what children bring to a writing task, the curriculum arrangements within which it occurs, and the principal dimensions of the writing, its aim, audience, content and mode.
>
> (Beard, 1984, p. 142)

An important first step is to consider the kinds of written work being done and the nature of the guidance and support that is offered. The range of writing tasks will be dependent on underlying assumptions about the aims and purposes for learning on which the curriculum is founded, and the ways in which these have been communicated to and understood by individual teachers.

All teachers, if we are to believe recent reports which suggest that 30% of time in the primary classroom is spent on writing activity, regard writing as important. Most would readily subscribe to a concern for the development of original ideas, for encouraging self-expression, for extending vocabulary and for enabling pupils to write fluently for pleasure and enjoyment. At the same time, teachers are anxious to lay the foundations of correct letter formation, of neat handwriting, to give every opportunity for the learning of grammar and punctuation, and to aim for improvements in the structure and style of writing. A comprehensive language policy, which stresses all these aspects of written language, exists in a majority of schools.

There are, however, significant differences in approach and emphasis. Traditional approaches tend to view writing as essentially concerned with communication, and clarity of thought and expression as vital if writing is to be of use in adult life. Classroom practices therefore operate within a common, restricted set of aims relating to the component skills, and comprise exercises and routine procedures with little opportunity for original writing. This system generates large quantities of print, and, as a consequence, copious amounts of marking; inevitably much of the teacher's time is spent on administration and little attention can be given to the actual processes of writing. The emphasis placed on the technical and clerical aspects of writing is communicated to children, who assess their development as writers in relation to a narrow range of school-learned skills.

The approach is based on a belief that all children can and will master the basic skills of writing and be able to cope with the writing demands of the curriculum. But the linguistic knowledge employed in writing is acquired rather than generated from within. It is not sufficient to have the technical skills; children also need to be explicitly taught about the aims and purposes of writing, particularly its relationship with reading, and encouraged to demonstrate increasing competence over a wide range of writing activity.

For teachers who believe this to be important, writing is a creative act – the exercise of the imagination in a search for personal growth and knowledge. Founded on the premise that children want to write, the teacher's aim is to build constructively on this natural urge. In the classroom, motivation is the key factor and the teacher regards the cultivation of positive attitudes to writing as a priority. If pupils are interested in writing and do not perceive it as fraught with difficulties, then they are more likely to be aware of its potential, and through indulging in writing, become confident in their own language and thought.

In such classrooms, teachers try to create a 'writing environment' in which the conditions for writing are deliberately contrived; where pupils do not necessarily all write at the same time; where they write because they have identified a genuine need for writing and where pupils exercise some freedom of choice in what to write and in how to write it. Much of the writing is done collaboratively, with children supporting one another and providing a critical audience for the writing. Their teachers respond to, rather than simply 'mark' the work, and quite often it reaches a wider audience, which might include children in other classes, parents or even be 'published' beyond the school community.

Not all that is intended however, becomes a reality. The general constraints that operate in schools and classrooms often mean that teachers are not free to make and present choices. They are obliged to teach within a necessary structure and framework, and problems of time, space, materials and resources can reduce the impact of a well-conceived programme. Administrative and organisational demands and requirements not infrequently cause teachers to resort to stylised routines and practices when implementing a writing programme. In their survey of pupil learning experiences, Bennett, Desforges, Cockburn and Wilkinson noted that:

> The predominant aim expressed in more than 70% of tasks intended to promote writing was to 'practice writing' and to use some aspects of grammar, especially capital letters and full stops as sentence markers.
>
> (Bennett *et al*, 1984, p. 101)

The child's experience

What then is the experience of pupils; what do they understand about writing and, as a consequence, what are their expectations? Much will depend on what the child brings to the task; writing will mean different things to different children according to their pre-school literary and linguistic experiences. The initial study of the Bristol Language Development Project (Wells, 1981a) indicated that almost every child, on entry to school, has mastered the basic meanings and grammar of the language of his community, and is engaging in a variety of interactions with people in his immediate surroundings. No child is completely non-verbal but there are enormous differences between children, from this basic threshold. This early learning occurs as the child attempts to find solutions to problems that are encountered in daily events and activities. Learning is more secure because it is child-directed and meets a need in a familiar context. The role of the adult in such learning is a supportive one, encouraging the child's attempts and acting as a resource for information and skill. The domestic situation encompasses all the important characteristics of successful learning.

A significant factor in later progress is the degree of congruence between home and school experience, and the extent to which the child has to cope with discontinuity. Follow-up studies of the project, which focused on the factors affecting success in the early years of schooling, concluded that the most important predictor of attainment at the age of seven years was the child's knowledge and understanding of the conventions of reading at the time of entry to school. Parents who read frequently to their children, encourage an interest in books and in reading and writing generally, provide this crucial background. The quality of everyday conversation is also important and for children who have had this early 'literary' grounding, differences between schools and methods of teaching are less significant in their overall development and attainment. What they have acquired is the ability to benefit from the more formal learning context of the classroom.

Issues and problems affecting performance

In the classroom, teachers have the task of identifying and building on the knowledge and abilities that children bring to school, while at the same time selecting and presenting curricular activities which meet broader educational objectives. It is a difficult balance to achieve, and for some children the situation is confusing and they do not understand what is expected of them, nor how to capitalise on what they already know. Children are learning about writing long before they come to school; they are surrounded by print in many forms and they are absorbing all kinds of information from it. Encounters with language, spoken and written, are part of every child's daily experience and the means by which they begin to make sense of the world about them. Crucially they come to realise that speech has a written equivalent and that adults use writing for a variety of purposes and in different ways. Few children will ever see adults (including teachers) writing at length, but most witness the occasional filling in of a form, the writing of a cheque, a scribbled message or the composing of a letter. They will be conscious of writing as a means of communication and aware of its functions in everyday life.

Too often there is little congruence between pre-school 'literary' experience, and that of the school, and inevitably, much of the early linguistic competence remains unexploited, particularly in relation to writing. It is, for the most part, regarded as almost exclusively school-taught. But as Hall has indicated,

> most children will arrive at school knowing something about what written language is, how it works and what it is used for.
>
> (Hall, 1987, p. vi)

The diversity of pupil response is also problematic for the teacher, and this may be one reason why, in so many classrooms, writing activities tend to conform to a pattern. The random character of pre-school writing is quickly absorbed into the picture/caption sequence that features in a majority of infant classrooms. This is a formula which readily transfers to first narrative writing, which is the model for the 'creative writing' or 'stories' of the later primary years.

For many children this is the typical sequence of learning about writing, and stories form the basic diet of their school writing experience – practised endlessly, always to a prescribed procedure, and often to the exclusion of other types of writing. It is not surprising that, for a significant number of children, the words, 'writing' and 'stories' are synonomous. Teachers need to be aware of the range of possible purposes to which writing may be put and in the most stimulating writing environments, teachers are presenting a variety of opportunities and challenges, and, over the course of time, increasing the demands for different types of writing. Children's own perceptions about writing in school, highlight for us some of the obvious and immediate problems, and incidently, testify to the complexity of the task.

> When you are doing writing it can be good when you have a good subject and a good teacher
>
> (boy, 10 years)
>
> I can never write well when told to write. I can only write when I want to. Sometimes I have a brilliant idea and then I find out that I have only a little time to write it and then I spoil it.
>
> (girl, 9 years)
>
> I write my best stories at school without a time limit and with a subject I like and when I'm not scared of the teacher. I do not like writing unless I have to. If I'm scared of the teacher I feel I have to do well but I am so anxious I do badly.
>
> (boy, 11 years)

These comments, made by articulate children who are already competent writers, suggest that there are some powerful constraints in operation in the classroom. Their views reaffirm the central role of the teacher, the importance of subject matter in directing and engaging interest, and reveal a considerable fear of failing to meet teacher expectation. The conditions for writing are clearly important and it would seem that the reality is far from ideal. Nevertheless, pupils do have compelling reasons for wanting to write and motivation does not appear to be a major problem.

> I think I would have liked to carry on writing some stories, but if I don't finish it then it's homework and I've got better things to do, so I rattle off a boring ending.
>
> (boy, 10 years)

If I'm enjoying a story I finish it properly. I usually choose (if it's a choice) the same sort of thing every time. I expect the teacher gets bored.

(girl, 10 years)

At home, before I came to school, my mum taught me how to write my name and what each letter in the alphabet sounded like . . . At school I never knew what to write and this stopped me writing more. I really wanted to write what I saw before I could write – things like fire engine, ambulance. I could always read what I had written. All this was very important.

(boy, 11 years)

The comments are necessarily subjective and difficult to quantify, but they do reveal some significant features of classroom practice which are hardly destined to promote either positive attitudes to writing or the desire to write from choice. It seems that the initial enthusiasm, perhaps fostered in the home, gradually tails off as the child becomes accustomed to the role of pupil.

It may be that in schools too much time is spent on learning to write, and on practising skills, with too little attention or time given to 'learning about writing', and in relating writing to all kinds of reading, and to other curriculum areas generally. A good deal of children's writing takes place outside the traditional language or English sessions, and the application of writing skills in a cross-curricular context has obvious benefits. It can, and does provide the opportunity to extend the range of types of writing children may attempt. In an environmental survey, in the re-telling of an historical event, in framing questions for research, in observing and recording the results of a scientific experiment, children have the opportunity to consider, confirm and shape their understanding.

Classroom organisation

This raises important questions in relation to classroom organisation and to the teacher's skill in integrating curriculum activity. Often there is relatively little integration within the language programme and topic or project writing tasks do not always give an opportunity to use existing skills and knowledge constructively. Integration of linguistic experiences is more likely to occur in the infant classroom, where the foundations of basic writing and reading skills are being laid, but it is not always evident in the junior classroom.

It may not, for example, be sensible to have all children writing at the same time. We are reminded that spelling requests constitute the bulk of teacher/pupil exchanges in writing periods (Bennett *et al*, 1984) at the expense of more profitable teacher support for the actual process. Although children clearly have to learn to cope with the systems and routines of the classroom (and there must be a structure to classroom organisation), there are substantial gains to be made in terms of independent learning in permitting children some freedom of choice in terms of content, length and style of writing. This is especially so with younger children for whom a written response is not always the most appropriate one. It is vital to draw on and extend the children's own offerings, to confirm what they can already do and its relevance in the classroom; to accept in the early years for example, language and syntax which does not correspond to adult notions and conventions, and in later years, to encourage individual and unconventional contributions.

Observation has shown that as pupils progress through their schooling, there is an increasing tendency to write for the teacher, typified by questions about the amount to be written, the time allowed for writing, for example. Pupils quickly learn to adapt their output to the requirements of the situation, as the Oracle (Galton, Simon and Croll, 1980) research has shown in its description of pupil types. In these circumstances writing is doing little for the writer, and the potential for self-expression, for creative thinking, is being lost. Composing becomes simply a process of filling time and a number of lines in an exercise book, and there is little opportunity for cognitive development. Genuine growth does not occur through drill and exercises.

Yet schools have the potential to engage pupils in a wide variety of writing activities across the curriculum, drawing on their skills in listening, speaking and reading and so extending the range of their linguistic competence. They write in order to clarify ideas and to relate new learning to existing experience. To each new learning situation the child brings knowledge, thoughts, feelings and experience. Their understanding of the situation and their freedom of manoeuvre within it, will profoundly affect their ability to respond. Progress is likely to be improved where the teacher makes conscious decisions about the context – in relation to the print displayed on the walls and to the resources of printed material available, in the opportunities created for writing and in the flexibility of response that is encouraged. Ideally, the classroom provides a situation in which pupils are encouraged to act as real writers, learning through writing, and working together to demonstrate their competence across subjects, activities and topics.

The National Writing Project

These are the issues which have been addressed by the National Writing Project, an intensive investigation of children's writing. As a starting point in 1985, a sample of teachers' observations about their classroom practice were analysed, prior to an examination of the ways in whch classroom practice might be modified to support and extend children's learning. The study has challenged many assumptions about pupils, classrooms, language and learning, and has contributed to our understanding of the complexities of the writing process. The conclusions are significant for classroom practice and performance, propounding a view of the child as actively involved in learning about language through a process of trial, error and adjustment. It therefore follows, it is argued, that language work in schools should arise naturally from pupils' own activity, in a context of real purposes and outcomes. With this approach, writing is not simply reduced to its components, but is part of a functional language system.

After three years of innovation and experiment, the National Writing Project has been influential in changing teachers' attitudes and expectations, changes which have been reflected in classroom practice. The project has provided evidence of the best of these practices to the National Curriculum Working Party on English, and the basic principles have been incorporated in the National Curriculum documents for English (DES 1989). In this respect, the National Writing Project has been instrumental in informing national policy and therefore in ensuring the widest possible dissemination of effective strategies and techniques in the teaching and development of writing. The impact is acknowledged thus:

> ... we have cause for optimism that changes in classroom practice have become institutionalised. Concepts such as writing for real purposes, for a variety of audiences and the interrelation of form and function have now become commonplace. Writing corners, role play and the valuing of

what children bring to the classroom are not only enshrined in our classrooms but also in legislation.

(National Curriculum Council,
About Writing Newsletter, No 11 Autumn 1989)

The National Writing Project has been the catalyst for far-reaching changes in thinking about writing; it has brought teachers together in support groups throughout the country, for the sharing of ideas and practice, and for maintaining progress and development. It is believed that where teachers are more acutely aware of the issues involved in writing, they can begin to consider alternative approaches.

The most effective way of developing classroom practice is by giving teachers the space to reflect, develop, discuss and share ideas and to try them out in a supportive environment.

(National Curriculum Council,
About Writing Newsletter, No 11 Autumn 1989)

CHAPTER 2

Towards a Theory of Writing Development

In trying to establish a structure for writing development, it is obvious that there is more involved in the learning of writing than simply mechanical translation skills. It is clear that to begin to understand how children learn to write we must go beyond the analysis of their writing samples (Clay, 1975), and actually observe children in the process of writing.

This approach was adopted by Bereiter and his colleagues, who encouraged children to talk about their understanding of writing and of the purposes it serves. The work of Bereiter and Scardamalia (1982) has particularly focused on 'procedural facilitation' – on those mental operations which appear to be most susceptible to facilitative intervention by sympathetic adults. Their research findings are therefore directed more towards the assessment and improvement of writing rather than towards a theory of development. But the research does detail points of reference about the writing process, and in the search for developmental features and general characteristics, draws upon a range of studies in which children emerge as active participants in the process of becoming writers. Most researchers are agreed that successful writing must ultimately synthesise intellectual, manual, artistic and creative capacities and energies. At different ages and stages there is likely to be variation in the cognitive load, and some elements in the process may be generally easier to deal with than others.

Of fundamental significance in any study of children's writing is the recognition that writing is only part of the complex web of language skills that includes talking, listening and reading. Development in writing will therefore be related to the utilising of wider linguistic potential. Writing also takes place within the broad context of the curriculum, and writing activities will be informed by progress and development in the growth of knowledge, ideas, skills and attitudes. All of this has major implications for classroom practice, for the nature and purpose of the writing curriculum, and for the evaluation and assessment of writing.

Pre-writing and the emergent writer

Research evidence inclines to the view that writing grows out of established oral patterns. Much of the pre-school child's use of language takes place in interaction, mainly with adults; the interaction providing the stimulus for talk, but perhaps also, in some circumstances, constraining language use. Those children who are exposed to a variety and complexity of interaction, who engage in conversations, and who talk about and share books, have a distinct advantage in terms of resources for writing, when they enter school. Research by Wells (1981a) has confirmed earlier observations that children bring to school a wide-ranging linguistic competence on which development in writing is based.

> Most children, by the time that they are ready to begin school, know the full contents of an introductory book in transformational grammer.
>
> (Brown, 1968, p.v.)

Nevertheless, there are critical differences between talking and writing and oral skills are not directly translated to the act of writing. In learning to write, as Kress observes:

> ...the stimulation of the interlocutor is missing. And whereas in speech the child creates a text in interaction, now he or she is, for the first time, forced to construct a text without the guide, the prodding, the stimulus of the interaction.
>
> (Kress, 1982, p. 35)

This imposes a different set of demands and the channelling of oral competence into writing is necessarily a complex operation. The abstract nature of writing means that the child has to become more self-sufficient, relying to an ever greater extent on personal resources. We are reminded by Thornton:

> A speaker can alter, cancel, start again. A writer can do this

at the drafting stage, but at some point he must let go of his writing . . . It is not, like spontaneous speech, inextricably bound to the context in which it occurs.

(Thornton, 1980, p. 27)

Nor can writing be achieved without the support of reading; they are mutually facilitating activities, dependent on a child's learning of the written symbols which represent words. Reading is a vital, additional resource and can stimulate and foster the desire to create images, and develop ideas in writing.

First writing may occur spontaneously, as do first utterances, but will involve several crucial psychological adjustments. It will probably take the form of what Vygotsky (1962) describes as 'meaningless and undifferentiated squiggles', but this is an essential symbolic development in the move towards conventional orthography. (Fig. 1)

The scribbles and marks of the pre-school child are, at first, quite random, but as the child gains skill in handling implements and

Fig. 1

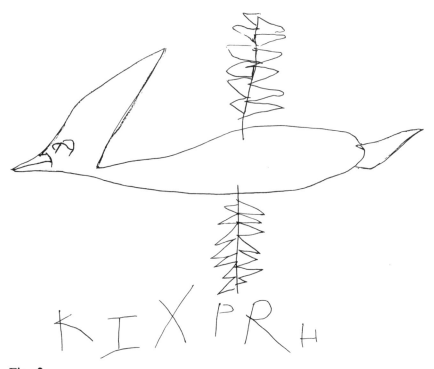

Fig. 2

conscious of the ability to 'create', drawing and writing gradually begins to take recognisable shapes and forms. Repetitive elements start to appear – recurring shapes and patterns, which suggest that conscious and deliberate choices are being made by the child. (Fig. 2)

In time, distinct letters and symbols are introduced; there is copying from books and other forms of print, and drawing and writing emerge as interchangeable, but separate activities. (Figs 3, 4)

Frequently there is a creative and imaginative combination of letter shapes and pictures, and eventually, more letters and symbols are incorporated into drawings. The quality of a child's drawing provides a valuable insight into the level of perception and the readiness to cope with the demands of writing.

At this stage, practice with a variety of implements, materials and media, the promoting of essential co-ordinatory skills and the linking of graphic and writing activities, will lay a basis for the development of communicative competence in speaking, writing and reading.

Pre-writing experience, while taking many forms, arises naturally out of a range of everyday domestic activity. It is also associated with

Fig. 3

Fig. 4

make-believe play and with 'pretend' writing and reading, where the pleasure of discovery in a personal response inculcates a desire for growth in self-knowledge. It all takes place in a situation free from evaluation, in which there is no 'correct' way to respond. These are significant factors when we consider the orthodox practices and conventions adopted in the teaching of reading and writing once the child is admitted to school. The National Writing Project, recognising the importance of pre-school writing experience, has been influential in nursery education, where, increasingly, emergent writing is being encouraged as part of the traditional structured play activities. It has been found that play may be productively extended by the provision of the opportunity for some form of 'writing' – the sending of messages, signing in at the start of the day, making shopping lists, for example. (Fig. 5)

Developmental writing in school

Just as many children come to school believing that they can read, so they will come willing to try to be writers. The very youngest children, given the opportunity to use what they know, are able to demonstrate considerable know-ledge of the forms and purposes of writing. This may at

Fig. 5 Reception class: message on telephone pad

first be simple 'draw writing' but as they develop and learn more about how written language works, their writing comes increasingly close to standard adult systems.

(*English for Ages 5 to 11*, D. E. S. 1988 10.12, p. 47)

First writing in school does not have to wait until the basic conventions of writing have been mastered. Pupils need the opportunity to experiment and to build up confidence in a new, and possibly unfamiliar situation. Characteristic features of this stage of development are associated with a recognition of the sounds and

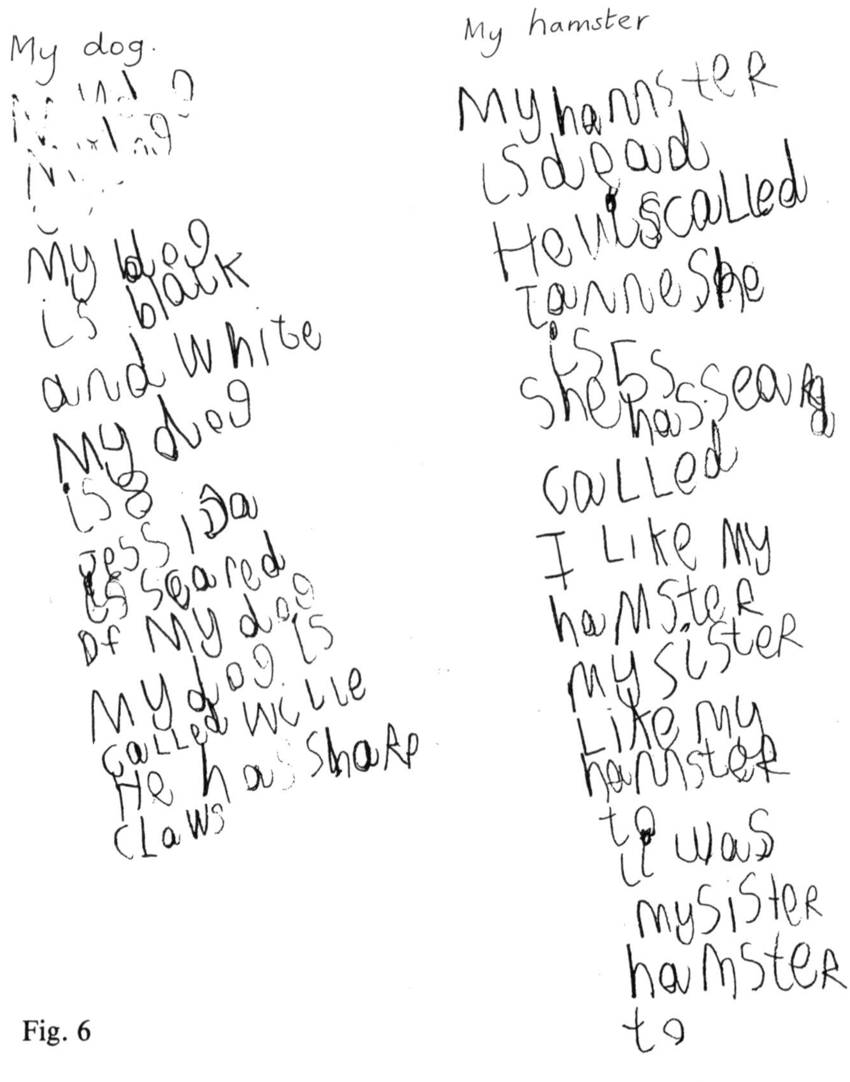

Fig. 6

shapes of letters, and with the beginning of understanding of how letters combine to make words. This is attended by an apparent need to register this information both visually and cognitively, and evident in the repeating of strings of letters which gradually approximate to words.

This absorbing and satisfying procedure was identified by Clay (1975) who refers to it as the 'inventory' principle. Ferreiro (1978a,b), in several studies of Mexican and Swiss children, claims that in children's early hypotheses about writing, conceptual identity usually predominated. It was also noted that there were three major limitations on the texts produced by children; a tendency to use a minimum quantity of letters (usually three); a restriction on the stock of letters known to the child; and an avoidance of repeating the same letter more than twice. This listing procedure is a necessary precursor to sentence and story writing. Children begin by putting together groups of words, in lines, often down one side of the page or sheet. (Fig. 6). The concept of a sentence is not understood at this stage and a child's first sentence is in fact a line of writing.

In his study of children learning to write, Kress (1982) describes the qualitative difference between the syntax of speech and writing in young children and examines the appropriateness of the form of the child's expression. First writing reads like and resembles speech, but because writing is a multi-faceted operation, the range of syntactic forms used in writing lag behind those commonplace in speech. In having to concentrate on other factors in writing, the use of syntax and textual structure is governed by what comes most readily to mind and imposes the least cognitive burden. For the young writer, the movements of speech are already well-organised, but the movements of writing are not. Writing, in effect, slows up the complex activity of synthesising information from memory and from different senses. This slowing-up may well be a prerequisite for progress, giving the child the chance to begin to control and master the necessary components.

There is evidence to suggest that early attempts to produce a detailed and differentiated script are an important indicator of intellectual development, showing rapid changes in thinking and conceptual flexibility. There are, of course, differences in perceptual sensitivity; we become familiar with the environment through our senses, and linking writing to other creative and expressive experiences could enhance potential. Indeed for most children, there seems to be a need to support early attempts at writing with a picture or diagram. This may indicate that many children need to visualise the content of their writing in order to effectively translate it into words and that there may be a lack of confidence in verbal description only. It might simply be a continuation of the widespread practice in infant classrooms, by which teachers encourage children to generate content for writing. The following procedures are typical:

(1) the child draws a picture, dictates a caption to the teacher, then traces over the caption as written by the teacher, (Fig. 7)
(2) the child draws a picture, dictates a caption and copies the caption written by the teacher,
(3) the child draws the picture and attempts to write the caption. (Fig. 8).

There may, of course, be problems of 'directionality' in these activities, especially where children are left unobserved or unsupported. But watching how the teacher constructs writing is part of learning about how to make a sentence. Although it is worthwhile to adopt this practice, it is inevitable that in the process of copying the teacher's writing, the content becomes less immediate and personal. There is no substitute for learning about writing through first-hand experience, though it has to be accepted that a good deal of information about writing will come through copying and experimenting with existing forms of print. In this respect, pre-reading

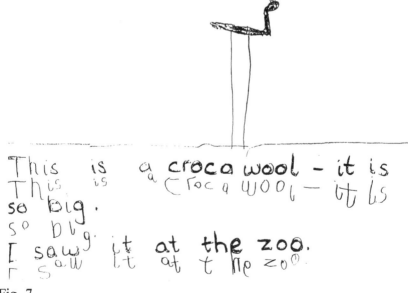

Fig. 7

Two dogs went for a walk to a cottage
They growled and then they went
back home.

Fig. 8

practices which are operating simultaneously can effectively support an understanding of left to right conventions. In laying the foundations for further development, it is important that writing should not be separated from other complementary activities. Practically all the activities which are part of the programme in the infant classroom, have the potential to generate some form of simple recording, and there is much that is child-initiated on which to capitalise. A growing aesthetic awareness in music, art, drama and movement will have a positive effect on the quality of writing.

Within the broader context of language development, children will need to hear lots of stories to help to establish the idea of a 'story grammar', and to learn the typicalities of writing, (i.e. formal beginnings and endings, the use of characters, events which share a time and space sequence) so that they can begin to differentiate between spoken and written language. It is far from certain that young children are aware of the relationship and connections between the different modes of language. This awareness has to be fostered; children are therefore encouraged to read their writing and to relate it to texts in books. In this way books, fiction and non-fiction, become a vital source of information about the purposes and power of writing.

The role that reading plays in the development of writing skills has to be considered. In speculating on the relationship between motor control and writing, Clay (1975) believes that there are physical reasons why writing must follow after the introduction of reading. Having to co-ordinate hand and mind forces a slow, careful analysis, bringing detail into focus in a way that may not happen in rapid reading. That reading and writing are interdependent activities is undeniable – older pupils who are poor readers are generally weak in writing performance. Although they may have the necessary motor control, recent theory suggests that they lack operations, strategies or plans for internalising and using word forms. As there appears to be a sequential order to the learning of these strategies, delay in, or inability to capitalise on these functions at the appropriate stage will have serious consequences for further progress.

Skills in reading and writing are generally prompted simultaneously in schools, for the most part building on pre-school experience. Beard has observed that children's expectations of reading and writing show similarities and differences. He notes that:

> For many children the abstract nature of written language is a source of doubt and uncertainty. The nature and importance of reading and writing activities are not clear to them.
>
> (Beard, 1984, p. 59)

This 'cognitive confusion' is also referred to by Downing (1969), who outlines practical activities such as talking about recipes and instructions which will strengthen understanding of the technical concepts of language. Writing may seem to children to be more immediately satisfying than reading, perhaps because the result is more directly observable and writing is easier to imitate than silent reading. In contrast to Clay's view, Graves (1975) proposes that a child's first urge is to write rather than to read, and that writing supports reading in bringing into use the auditory, visual and kinaesthetic skills which contribute to it. Waiting for children to be quite fluent readers before encouraging them to write is, argues Wells (1981b), to miss valuable opportunities for extending interest in writing. If manual dexterity and language facility are promoted within a broad context of reading and writing activity, the growth of early writing skills is established. The years four to seven can be seen as a period in which the first representational attempts are made – the beginning of graphic communication and the conscious creation of form.

The beginning of narrative

Even before they are able to write, some children are able to dictate stories which have the qualities of written rather than spoken language. For a majority of children, however, progress in writing is largely through narrative. By seven years of age, most children can write what approximates to a sentence, but have not necessarily acquired an understnading of a story framework or schema. Their writing therefore, corresponds to talk; it is a loosely structured list of events, usually sequential but with inconsistencies in the tenses. It contains familiar story phrases and conventions, such as 'once upon a time' and 'they all lived happily after'. Invariably the events take place in a familiar domestic setting, within the space of a day and draw to a

Looking after a dragon for a weekend

Once upon a time there lived a boy called James. He was a kind and hceted boy. Anyway one day he heard a terrific (noun) coming from outside. He went over to the window and say a dragon I was so surprised my eyes nearly poped out.

James (Aged 7)

36

Not long ago in a place called Noddy Land Where king Noddy lived and ruled. One day the royal family had a (babby) baby Son. years went by and there Son was now the age of Nine, he was growing repe(i)dly. One day when the prince was very (board) bored and had nothing to do he decided to have a walk in the palace garden's. He went and sat on a bench feeling very sorry for him-self.

Madeline (Aged 7)

close at bedtime. There is minimal description and few, if any, explanations for actions or events.

According to Beard (1984) the production of writing may be seen as comprising three basic components: 'composing, transcribing and reviewing.' The intricate nature of their relationship has been examined in recent years, but no satisfactory conclusive evidence has been offered to support a complete and systematic explanation.

Transcription has possibly received more attention in educational studies, but the composing process is the real heart of the matter. The problem is one of gaining access to the 'data' to begin to identify the different cognitive processes which are engaged. From their observations of pupils in the act of writing, Bereiter and Scardamalia (1982) confirm that learning to write involves a change from oral to graphic expression; from face-to-face communication to communication with a remote audience; from dependence on a reciprocal 'conversation partner' to the development of a system of communication which can function independently and autonomously.

Kroll (1983) describes four phases in the acquisition of writing capability, namely: preparation, consolidation, differentiation and integration. The phases are not discrete periods, but represent a progression along a developmental continuum, and it is not easy to assign chronological ages to their onset. It is reasonable to suppose. argues Perera (1984), that the consolidation stage begins at about six or seven years, and the differentiation stage at about nine or ten years. She bases her evidence for the onset of the latter stage on those studies which reveal that grammatical structures rarely found in speech tend to appear in the writing of pupils in the last two years of junior schooling.

At about seven years of age children are beginning to take the first tentative steps towards autonomy in writing; the basic mechanisms and techniques of orthography and spelling have been acquired and during this period of consolidation, children write as they speak. Inevitably the immaturities of speech are transferred to writing and there is rarely any attempt to re-read or alter, but there is now some evidence of deliberation in the stories that are taking shape. Writers are now able to attend to the spacing between words, to linear organisation and to the shaping of the writing on the page. Nevertheless, children find it difficult to maintain consistency, and in attending to the secretarial aspects of writing, have less concentration to invest in composing the content for writing. Progress is therefore recursive, with advances in dealing with the component skills being paralleled by a loss of quality in the content.

The emphasis in schools on the production of a neat script might further block progress by concentrating a child's energies unproductively. The reluctance of some children to write may well spring from an inability to master basic handwriting skills; the use of a tape recorder or word processor will often reveal that the problem is not a lack of content.

Children will become increasingly independent at different rates, but once a child has gained assurance in its capacity to reproduce words accurately, and has begun to construct sentences, attention can then

Tyres   Thursday 22 Janvery 87
and treads

We got some rubber And pushed the rubber over
Some bord and we found out what it felt like
And then We cut three treds And We pushed it
along the Bord And the rubber gript more. then
We tried the overside of the Bord And the rudder gript
more then tn over side. thenWe put Some Water over
The Bord . And pushed the rubber over the Water and
The rudder sidded threw the water . then We put oil
on the Bord and it Just slid along .

Fig. 9

focus on content and on the combining and relating of sentences to develop a topic or theme. This will involve generating knowledge about a particular topic, selecting from it, framing a response and finally, choosing the appropriate register to meet the requirements of the task. In the early stages of narrative writing, the child is unable to deal with register, so that even when asked to write a report or to record an activity or event the written products will read as stories. Objectivity is difficult to achieve although there will be children who are beginning to vary their response according to the task. (Fig. 9).

For most pupils however, writing experience will centre on narrative; stories form the basic diet as they learn about the conventions of writing and of the rules that govern the system. Indeed, narrative writing appears to have a specific function in the development of children's writing;

> Narrative writing may thus have a specially important place in the learning of writing, in that it permits the child to develop textual structures and devices in writing by drawing on the child's already established abilities in spoken language.
>
> (Kress, 1982, p. 59)

It is chiefly in the content of narratives that characteristic features are immediately obvious, because pupils continue to write about what is most familiar to them and draw on their own immediate experience. (Fig. 10). Some common themes and topics emerge, and the critical importance of parents, siblings, friends, pets and toys is evident; the author has a central role in relation to these familiar others, and writing assumes a high level of intimacy on the part of the reader. Food is a recurring theme and is invariably described in some detail. The setting is most often domestic, with parties, outings, and school providing the background.

Despite the inclusion of conventional story phrases, some of the language structures used regularly in speech do not show up in writing until perhaps around ten years of age. Perera (1984) notes a relationship between maturity in speech and in writing; until about nine years of age there is generally a lower level of grammatical maturity in writing than in speech, even though writing at six, seven and eight years of age is an extension and reflection of speech patterns and forms. The issue of spelling is also significant, and words that a child may use confidently and competently in speech may not appear in writing until a later stage.

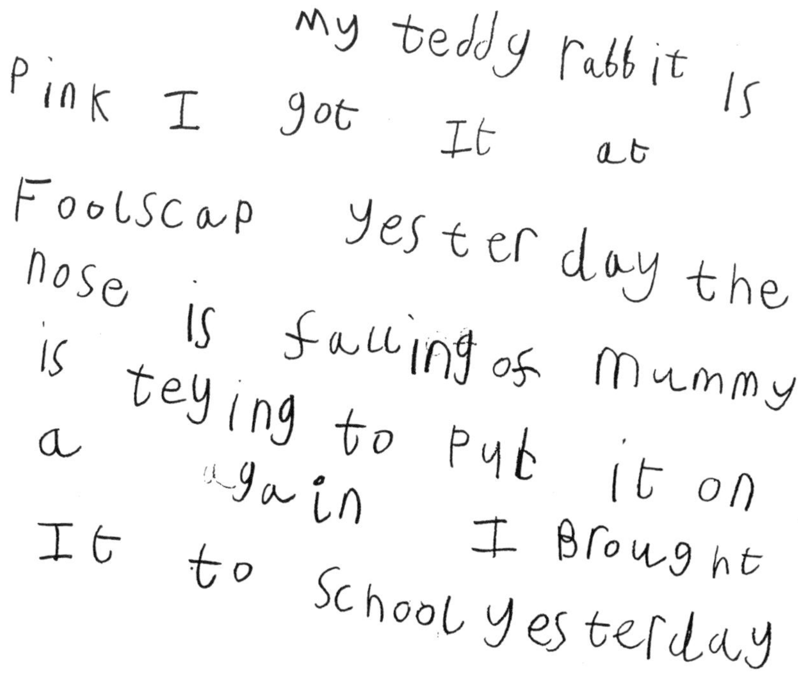

My teddy rabbit is
Pink I got It at
Foolscap yesterday the
nose is falling of mummy
is teying to put it on
a again I Brought
It to School yesterday

Fig. 10

Although research (Peters, 1970, Dunsbee and Ford, 1980) indicates that in the acquisition of spelling skills, visual perception, verbal intelligence and carefulness are the key factors for success, performance in spelling is also linked to the cultural background of the home. Substantial pre-school experience of books and writing lays a foundation on which schools can build in training pupils in ways of looking at and learning words.

Growth in understanding of form and structure

Between nine and eleven years, writing is recognised as a distinct and separate form, partly as a result of schooling and of teaching practices. Bereiter (1980) observes that as soon as we begin to investigate the functional aspects of pupils' writing, we discover more about school practices than we learn about the child. This might indicate that one of the reasons why writing is not commensurate with speech in the early years in school, is that opportunities to utilise oral linguistic potential in writing are ignored or not fully exploited. Class writing tasks may not sufficiently encourage speculation, questioning, projecting and deduction, but tend to predispose pupil responses to the narrative mode.

On entry to school, it is not unreasonable to assume that speech has become automated into thinking. Writing necessarily demands further deliberation and regression can be expected. In the development of speech there are periods of instability, as new words are learned and different language structures and strategies are employed; so in writing, the complex co-ordination of activities redefines priorities and as a consequence, ideation may occupy a smaller portion of cognitive power. Scardamalia (1981) considers that the process of planning and reviewing may be relatively late to develop in young children because they already have so much to attend to in terms of spelling, selection and use of vocabulary, punctuation etc. as well as mastering the skills of handwriting.

Writing serves a crucial function in relation to cognitive development. It allows for the examination, exploration and development of ideas – once an idea has been written down it is possible to examine it objectively. Writing encourages the generation of ideas which are not transient as those in speech, and rapid progress appears to be made after nine years of age when a higher proportion of complex constructions are introduced, including some which rarely occur in spontaneous speech. These constructions eventually enter the child's spoken language, suggesting that as pupils become more literate, writing acts as a stimulus to overall linguistic development, enabling words, phrases and constructions to be filtered through the medium of writing.

The impact of reading is also significant at this stage, when pupils are beginning to be aware of what Vygotsky (1962) refers to as the 'abstract quality of written language'. He addresses the difficulties inherent in dealing with abstraction, pointing to grammar and writing as ultimately enabling a child to rise to a higher level of speech development. The psychological significance of representing language in a permanent form should not be underestimated. The art of transcription lies not simply in a direct application of the knowledge and skills of language, its sounds, words and grammars. Key cognitive adjustments are related to changes in perceptions of language when speech is transcribed into written forms.

The subtle changes in awareness and understanding of language, though difficult to quantify, are gradually absorbed into writing. The effects are most immediately seen in the shaping and structuring of writing as pupils recognise and respond to the need to revise and re-draft, and to consider appearance as well as content.

This stage of development corresponds to the child's recognition of a reader and the realisation that this imposes certain obligations if the writing is to make sense and be acceptable. A perception of a reader is a key facet of the child's development as a writer. With younger pupils, the more abstract the task the more difficult they find it to decentre and they encounter problems of labelling versus naming, tending to partial information in their confusion as to what will make sense to the reader. For this reason, much of the writing of seven year olds is characterised by a preoccupation with self. Inevitably, there are classroom practices which impose additional burdens on the pupils in this period, not least the necessity to produce neatly scripted writing at the expense of interesting ideas, which are well-constructed and logically developed.

The features now entering children's writing demonstrate a gradual move from a totally centric role to that of an observer. The beginning of characterisation is reflected firstly in the personalising of inanimate objects, still within a fairly restricted and familiar context, but there is some evidence of the exploration of causal relationships and outcomes. As control of the linear structure is extended, there is a more secure handling of the sequence of events and the complexity of the plot increases. Some attempt is being made to plan a piece of writing as a whole, but the problem of sustaining and developing an idea or theme is evident in long introductions with minimal development to follow. This may imply that retaining interest is difficult where the mechanics of writing consume much of the time and energy. For many pupils an interest in illustrations appears to be strong at this stage, and sustained texts are quite often punctuated by drawings or patterns. It may be that some pupils are not convinced that they can rely on words alone to adequately convey their meaning or intentions, and resort to illustrations as a means of strengthening the text – a format familiar to them in reading books. There is also an interest in presenting the writing in chapters, children often making a concentrated effort to sustain the writing over several days or even weeks. Coupled with this interest in illustrations is the suggestion of humour and a wish to entertain the reader. This direct response to a reader suggests that the child has the beginnings of self-confidence as a writer, and has understood that writing is for reading. (Fig. 11).

The Battle of the Bloodstream

It was a busy day in the Bloodstream
Red cells racing about.
White cells guarding entrances,
And the steady beat of the heart.

But suddenly there was a bang.
And then a great big crash.
A bang and a crash and a huge great
                                    smash.

And germs were breaking in!!

The white cells were called from their
                                    posts.
Red cells ran to the germ-shelters.
Arms were grabbed, Germs were nabbed
And the battle raged thick and fast.

Meanwhile, outside,
The suffering boy,
Saw the mosquito flying away,
He said "Oh damn! Oh heck!
Where is that blomin' fly spray.

Fig. 11

The development of meaning and intent

All this would appear to confirm the findings of the Crediton Project; that the main dimensions of cognitive maturity from seven to thirteen years lie in a greater capacity for generalising information and decentring. The ability to describe, interpret, predict and speculate improves with age, enabling language to be more securely controlled and manipulated. In theory, meaning and intention in writing should become increasingly explicit, and the writer confident in choosing the appropriate style and register. How far this is related to the nature of the task is difficult to assess; few pupils at thirteen, for example, would be unable to report a simple sequence, though a fair proportion of seven year olds are unable to do so. In the Crediton project one of the tasks set out to test pupils' ability to justify an opinion explicitly in writing. Less than a third of seven year olds were able to assess their position, and offered restricted reasons to justify the argument – the majority produced descriptions, partial information dominating their accounts. Assessment, reasoning and deduction were all present in a majority of accounts at ten years of age, and by thirteen, a majority could not only assess and evaluate attitudes, but also attempted to make their own logic explicit. Nevertheless, coherent organisation is still difficult at ten, though it is well-established by thirteen.

Harpin (1976) found few examples of tentativeness or hypothesizing in his research with nine to eleven year olds, yet they emerged consistently in the writings of ten year olds in the Crediton sample. The difference must lie in the type of assignments set for the pupils, and this is clearly significant in relation to classroom practice. The nature of the task affects its outcomes, and cognitive development is enhanced where pupils have the opportunity not only to write about what they know and understand, but also to try to explain what is less accessible. The prelogical explanations of the early years give rise to circumstantial and restricted reasoning chains in the later junior years. This in turn leads to the ability to hypothesize, to imagine other possibilities and alternatives, and to generalise accordingly.

Once pupils are aware that writing can be shaped and altered to suit specific purposes, they can begin to concentrate on the differing requirements of structures other than the story form. The setting out of personal letters, or writing in verse or rhyme, can pave the way for experimenting with the organisation of non-chronological writing such as description, argument and explanation. The ordering of information still poses problems, possibly because the child now has more to say and is also concerned to meet the needs of the reader. There is also the question of the relevance and selection of information. Equally important is the choice of vocabulary, which will in part be determined by the content and requirements of the writing. A child's vocabulary is continuously developing although the rate of acquisition will vary considerably from child to child. It is highly individual and personal, influenced by and fed from many sources, but especially enriched by extensive reading. Exhortations to use a wider, more interesting vocabulary only make sense to a child if examples are provided, and there is regular attention, through a range of cross-curricular activity to the range and appropriateness of vocabulary, so informing the choices to be made.

That conscious choices are being made at about nine years of age is seen in the general increase in liveliness of pupils' writing.

At this stage the more mature writers move deliberately towards the creation of atmosphere, and begin to take advantage of descriptive writing to introduce sights and sounds, and there is altogether more vitality and action in the finished products. Activities and events are moving beyond their immediate surroundings and some limited ability to control variation in scene, time and place is apparent. At times there is an almost excessive use of dialogue, some stories consisting entirely of conversation. The implication is that the distinction between

LOOKING BACK

Looking back at J1 I have had lots of different experiences. It was my first year in the juniors and I have enjoyed it very much. I made new freinds in J1 such as: Nicola and Megan. Nicola came half way through the year and Megan came at the begining of the year. I have made quite good progress in marbles and I like the game, but the trouble is some people will not play with me because they say that I am too good. Anyway I still have lots of other people to play. I am trying desprately to catch up with Anna in maths, she is incredible, she works really fast, and it is impossible to catch up with her! I am going up to J3 next year and I am looking forward to it.

Looking after a dragon for a weekend

"Help, Rachael!" Screamed Nicola, running out of the cave. "What is it?" I asked. "Come and look". she replied.

In the cave, sitting on a rock, was a small dragon. "We can't leave it here", she whispered "It'll drown at high tide". So we decided to take it home. "There is no point in telling anybody." I said, trying unsuccessfully to get the dragon into my beach-bag. "Why not?" asked Nicky. If someone said to you "Hey, I just found a dragon," would you believe them?" "Well, er, no, I suppose. Here, try feeding him, them maybe he'll go into the bag". suggested Nicola.

Rachael (Aged 11)

speaking and writing is now entirely clear and is being explored and reinforced through frequent practice.

More obvious evidence of developing cognitive competence is the introduction of elements of abstraction and conjecture. Modifications in the structure and syntax in deference to the reader are attempted, but perhaps the most interesting and unexpected feature, is the inclusion of moral lessons in which the writer distinguishes between good and bad. There are no existing studies in which children's writing has been analysed for levels of moral thinking, but Wilkinson (1980) argues for the inclusion of a model for moral development in the Crediton project on the grounds that the development of moral thought parallels, and is related to, general cognitive development. Both Piaget (1932) and Kohlberg (1963, 1964), emphasise some type of stage concept, some notion of age-linked sequential reorganisation in the development of attitudes, and relate development in moral judgement to the process of decentring in thinking. Common sense and psychological studies tell us that 'growing up' is attended by decentring – of self towards others and in relation to reality. It is also accompanied by changes in attitudes and in the judgements made about oneself, others and reality, in the light of greater understanding.

Writing as a process of self-discovery

In examining the dynamics of the central components of the writing process, there is, inevitably, an emphasis on ways of thinking. There is the attendant assumption that there is a direct link between written language and cognition. It is vital nevertheless to acknowledge that a number of other important factors are influential in determining progress and development. The writer's values, motivation, self-concept and knowledge and ideas about the world will also be significant in terms of inclination and interest. These affective aspects of personality, which dictate emotional and imaginative responses, cannot be totally disassociated from cognition. Ways of feeling are not ultimately independent of ways of thinking, but while there may be consensus about development in cognition, it is less easy to establish a hierarchy of ways of feeling.

The engaging of the emotions becomes evident in writing at about 10 years of age when writing becomes more expressive as pupils seek ways in which to convey affect in writing. Writing is after all, a process of discovery as well as a communication of what is known. Arguably it is this process of discovery, as manifest in writing, that enables us to chart cognitive development. This advance in self-knowledge and personal growth has three dimensions: self, others and reality, and is demonstrated in a move from total interest in self towards empathy with others within the framework of a physical and social world. It can perhaps be assumed to parallel a cognitive advance in coping with the same capacity to shift perspective and to handle greater distances as well as points of view, in time and space, between the writer, the reader and experience. As in Moffett's (1968) hypothesis, a child develops the ability to move from the present and particular to the abstract and hypothetical. Britton (1975) reiterates the significance in writing of the growth in the sense of audience and 'the ability to make adjustments and choices in writing which take account of the audience for whom the writing is intended.'

Writing need not therefore be judged only in terms of success in content, presentation and organisation, but for what it reveals about the writer's emotional development and sense of reality. When children first start writing they are quite unselfconscious in their role as narrator. Once fully conscious of this role, writing is constructed for and around the perceived needs and demands of the audience. But to convey affect in writing is more difficult than in speech, especially for young children who do not have a range of stylistic devices or metaphorical language on which to draw. Consequently, their writing may not represent the child's total linguistic resources. In exploring the connections between language and the process of writing, thinking and perceiving, it becomes apparent that it involves the integration of skills and knowledge from several intellectual domains; the textual (aspects of language), the referential (objects, actions, events), the communicative (judgements about audience, adequacy of the message etc.). Importantly it involves the construction of new cognitive modes of organising the world, in which affective aspects will be instrumental.

At about seven years of age, writing contains literal statements with no affective elements – feelings are not explicitly expressed. It may be that a concern with the basic mechanics of writing precludes an awareness of writing as a means of extending imagination and understanding. It is probable that a preoccupation with the 'self' dimension, is an important prerequisite in the representation of a 'story world' which others will eventually inhabit. It is the process, Britton believes, by which:

> ...we construct a representation of the world as we experience it, and from this representation, this cumulative record of our own past, we generate expectations concerning the future, expectations which, as moment by moment the future becomes the present, enable us to interpret the present.
>
> (Britton, 1970, p. 14)

A gradual fusion of affective and cognitive elements allows the child at about ten years to be more explicit about emotions (though not to be introspective), and to introduce in their writing other people who are beginning to express thoughts and feelings. By thirteen years the process is apparently well-advanced, with themes showing greater psychological authenticity and objectivity. At this stage, recognition of self, others and reality is fixed in consciousness and confidence in a personal way of telling or recording enables connections to be made between differing perceptions and perspectives. These features will be appearing in the writing of able pupils from about ten years of age. In a longitudinal framework which sets out five basic stages in writing, Bereiter (1980) in focusing on the process, the product and the reader, emphasises the integration of cognitive and affective elements that is taking place. There is no guarantee that the product will explain the process, but the qualitative and expressive aspects will be the tangible evidence of the existing cognitive resources.

Development in cognition and affect

The following developmental model is proposed:

COGNITIVE ⟨————————⟩ WRITER ⟨————————⟩ AFFECTIVE	
Describing Naming Partial information Recording Reporting	Literal statements Environment assumed
Interpreting **Self** Explaining Inferring Deducing	Own emotion expressed, implied; Evaluates emotion; Interprets reality in terms of fantasy; Partial information on environment,
Generalising Abstracting Summarising Overall evaluation Concluding Reflecting Classifying **Others**	Awareness of others, some perceptions of others' feelings and thoughts; Interpretive comment on aspects of character; Recognition of and catering for a reader; Interprets reality literally in terms of logical possibilities; Responds to environment.
Speculating Irrelevant Relevant Hypothesis Exploring Projecting Theorising **Reality**	Awareness of physical, social world; Sense of time/place; Interprets reality imaginatively in terms of art, perhaps symbolically, metaphorically; Consistent realised presentation of another person; Ability to see others in an extended context.

Although a tentative model and far from conclusive, it emerges directly from the published findings of the Crediton Language Development Project. In tracing development it assumes, for example, that describing is less difficult than speculating; that there are stages in coping with abstraction which are relevant to generalising and speculating. It is a model which could reveal whether or not a child is repeating established patterns of thought, trying out new schema or attempting to translate experience competently and coherently. It is possible that children shift to a new hypothesis when their current theory conflicts with new experience, and the power of making and improving on a statement acts as reinforcement.

Goodnow (1977) and Ferreiro (1978) offer evidence of this facility in writing, while Duckworth (1979) offers a Piagetian statement of explanation which links affective and cognitive responses. He suggests that where a child has a theory, no matter how naive, instances which confirm or contradict that theory will be noted, with contradiction leading to a re-formulation of the theory.

Implicit in his theory of developmental change is the notion that where the child is the originator, he is likely to have a greater commitment and take more responsibility for formulating ideas in a manner which is clear and explicit enough for others to understand. At seven, children structure stories out of awareness of the story form, their own experience, their feelings and the language they use most effectively. The young child is motivated to make sense of the world, but is without the cognitive strategies to cope with non-fiction writing with its emphasis on logic and meaning – they write simply about what is of interest to them. By ten, they are more in control of the medium and can begin to explore its potential and further experience calls for continuing reorganisation. In subsequent years, this active processing of information enables children to operate on problems and by means of hypothesis, speculation and projection, achieve their own solutions and construct new meanings.

It is argued that affective development can only be considered objectively when related to cognitive development. That the joint model presented here is not entirely arbitrary may be inferred from those psychological studies which indicate that personal growth is attended by 'decentring'; of self towards others and in relation to reality. This decentring is first reflected in speech, where emotions are conveyed directly through face-to-face contact and through gesture; in writing, expressive qualities are dependent on the mastery of a range of stylistic devices, which are acquired, developed and controlled only with cognitive maturity.

The emergence of style

Whereas the cognitive and affective aspects of writing pose theoretical and practical problems, a developmental progression in style is more immediately accessible. Nevertheless, little research has been done in this field, presumably because although it is possible to identify constructions that are characteristic of written language, it is not possible to be precise about their effects. Such studies as do exist tend to examine measurable trends rather than focus on the stylistic function of particular constructions. But if we can accept that style has its origins in the simple, literal statements of the young child, then a theory of development can be based on what Wilkinson describes as:

> ... the choices which are made in relation to the norm of sentence in terms of syntax and vocabulary; choices of structure and level of abstraction; choices of metaphor and effect; choices of audience and overall choices in terms of writer's intentions.
>
> (Wilkinson, 1980, p. 45)

In isolating style as a developmental feature there is the danger of viewing it as a separate entity and unrelated to other aspects of growth. Style will inevitably be an integral part of expression, implying that stylistic features cannot be considered without reference to the cognitive and affective aspects of writing. As Bereiter points out:

> Attaining a degree of mastery over stylistic conventions leads in turn to the discovery that writing can be used to affect the reader – that it can direct, inform, amuse, move emotionally, and so on.
>
> (Bereiter, 1980, p. 89)

He goes on to argue that once this mastery has been achieved, it feeds back to the writer, establishing "a kind of dialogue with oneself" which leads not only to improved writing but also to improved understanding.

In this period of development, which tends to occur around ten and eleven years of age, there is a considerable increase in vocabulary as pupils strive to develop the imaginative content. This is supported by more evidence of global planning so that the writing is more

The Cat Hunter

...........The cat slinks through the small gap of the kitchen door. His sly

eyes watch as he prowls through the finely mown grass wishing it was

twice as tall as himself.

He moves swiftly and slenderly watching the tree.

The birds twitter. They know the danger but do the nestlings.

He moves his head up and down getting ready to pounce.

A young bird falls. It's in a panic, and pounce! The cat is upon the bird.

With a final sound the bird is dead and the cat drops it by the door.

Laura (Aged 11)

thoroughly and competently organised, and attention is given to the ending as well as the beginning of the writing. In stories, endings are less abrupt, and more creatively accomplished.

Pupils are now keen to develop the potential of paragraphs in the organising of writing, and a knowledge of the lay-out of books, both fiction and non-fiction is permeating texts. The content of stories is improved by the capacity to write from differing perspectives and to sustain extended viewpoints, and the ability to write objectively is now confidently exploited in scientific writing, reports and reviews, and with increasing competence in poetry and the writing of plays. A balance between dialogue and narrative has now been achieved and there is a marked advance in knowledge of the different conventions in writing. This means that pupils have the option to choose the most appropriate register or format for their writing, and in this respect, they begin to show evidence of their wider reading.

The most able pupils will be able to reproduce the style of a favourite author, and will begin to experiment with metaphorical language and with other literary devices. At times this may appear to be incongruous or over-elaborate, but in the creation of an original piece of writing, it is an essential stage in the development of the imaginative and poetic use of language.

Narratives in particular, show a maturity and sensitivity. There is much fuller characterisation, and in developing and describing people, young writers offer convincing portrayals of adults and other children, with a recognition of their actions, attitudes and behaviour. Some children are particularly alert and sensitive to the feelings of others, and can deal effectively with quite emotive issues. The introduction of aggressive and argumentative incidents in narratives is further evidence of the capacity to deal with wider views and opinion, and to argue a case.

The use of well-known idioms is creeping in and there is also increasing use of a colloquial vocabulary.

At this stage it is possible to begin to distinguish between the writing of girls and boys, as they adopt specific styles and characteristics. An almost clinical, factual approach is used by boys, who generally aim for a more succinct and concise style than that favoured by girls.

Organisational resources and methods

But style will not emerge simply as a result of the use of a varied vocabulary, mature sentence structure or the careful planning and organisation of writing – though in many cases this will produce good, satisfactory writing. It draws on a considerable range of cognitive and linguistic resources in a general movement from partial to complete organisation of writing. A conscious attention to style in writing represents a significant developmental characteristic and signifies a capacity to select from a repertoire as appropriate. It reveals a child's ability to plan, organise and manipulate language and ideas in graphic form. Once a piece of writing has been completed we can only infer the composing process that went into it. Examination of its structure, syntax, vocabulary and cohesion ought to give some indication of the stage of development reached in communicating successfully. Progression appears to follow a pattern which can be briefly summarised as follows:

(1) early writing adopts the narrative style where other registers are more appropriate;

(2) there is an increase in sophistication, especially in terms of time shifts;

(3) cognitive development is evident in the emergence of other organising systems, e.g. logical, classificatory;

(4) there is a growing awareness of the variety of forms available together with knowledge of the necessary code, though

consistency may vary with the difficulty of the task;
(5) a greater control over syntax and cohesion becomes apparent with a consequent interest in affect as well as content:
(6) there is more exact use of words, idioms and of dialogue;
(7) there is evidence of experimenting with 'literary' language.

Command of, and control over written language takes time and effort, involving the co-ordination of manual, artistic and intellectual skills. Kress observes that

> Much of the success in achieving full command of the written language rests on the child's mastery of the concept of sentence on the one hand and of the genres in which written language occurs on the other.
>
> (Kress, 1982, p. 61)

Grammatical and conceptual development

The sentence is not a unit of spoken language, and in first writing, the child grapples with syntax in a bid to produce a written sentence. Kress (1982) believes that textual, rather than syntactical units are produced first, and writing fills a line or space. The first major advance is for the child to establish what constitutes a sentence. Further cognitive demands arise in recognising its function as a constituent unit of a text, and of its specific place within a larger text.

There is further strong evidence (Britton, 1970, Wilkinson, 1980) to support the view that narrative has a powerful cognitive and conceptual impact on the child, laying the foundation for progress and development in writing. The demands of non-narrative writing are much greater, both cognitively and linguistically:

> It might be said that in narrative writing events control the writer, whereas in non-narrative writing the writer has to control events.
>
> (Kress, 1982, p. 78)

A significant phase in writing development has been reached when a child consciously begins to exercise this control, and is able to impose an alternative order.

Generally, short, complex sentences containing brief modifying phrases are typical of this stage. There is frequent use of adverbial clauses of time and place while clauses of cause and condition, although used, are not firmly established. Syntax, in all its essential characteristics is probably secure by the age of twelve. Perera (1984) claims that children below nine years of age, have a lower level of grammatical maturity in writing than in speech, and confirms that it is at about nine, that writing is recognised as separate and distinct from speech.

This phase is marked by first attempts in achieving stylistic effects, a facility noted in the Crediton Project. In the study, the researchers observed that children were beginning to rearrange particular units within a sentence, choosing longer, more complex sentences for effect. There was also the emergence of a less personal style in discursive writing. Most children, by this stage, have control over the mechanics and techniques of writing and can therefore begin to indulge in experiments in style. Perera (1984) and Kress (1982) both comment on the new relation between speech and writing that occurs at this time. Syntactical competence now provides the framework for the embedding of clauses, and allows for greater elaboration of concepts and the hierarchical organisation of ideas.

Further substantial progress is made in relation to the organisation of sentences within the whole composition. the internal consistency already established in sentence structure is now imposed on the use of paragraphs. The paragraph becomes the unit that contains topically-connected material, and supports a closer integration within sentences. Between ten and thirteen years of age, writing is conceived more as a whole, so that introductions and conclusions are confidently employed. This in turn supports the development of an impersonal style within new modes of textual and conceptual organisation. This initial process of decentring is associated with the writer's recognition of a reader, and, for a time, the need to explain and elaborate for a reader may limit the freedom the writer perceives in terms of conceptual and textual development. Control of the text and the ability to employ stylistic devices in a more deliberately expressive manner gives the writer a measure of control over the reader.

Eventually content becomes more important than the need to cater for a reader, and as a consequence, writing acquires an increasingly formal, impersonal and abstract character. This capacity to respond appropriately and effectively, and to communicate in less overt and obvious ways, marks an important advance in understanding of the nature of writing. (Fig. 12).

Nevertheless, of central importance in creating a cohesive text, which has point and purpose, is the extent to which the various parts of the text are related to the overall theme. A crucial factor in developing

ow Winter and Summer had a younger brother and sister and they to had heard the arguements and decided to inquire.

They listened to to Summer who said "Winter says that as he is older he should be the first season to start the New Year, but I don't think that's fair."

Then they listened to Winter who said the oppisite to Summer.

ery soon the Brother and Sister spoke again:

"We have decided that Winter will start his season in November and go on through until January then I, Spring will take over in February and go on until April. Summer will start in May and go on until July and I, Autumn will go from August on till October and then we start again.

Fig. 12

writing competence is the ability to generate and expand ideas within an organised structure. But different forms of writing require different structural components, and Hoey (1979) has indicated that, as a rule, the following elements are contained in writing: situation, problem, solution, result, evaluation. Early narrative writing typically consists of a setting, followed by a series of events and sometimes a conclusion, though these tend to be problematic. Growing maturity is reflected in the inclusion of all the necessary components and in the deliberate choices and placing of stylistic devices to create, elaborate and expand a structurally harmonious text.

Perera (1984) concludes that few trends can be associated with the development of clause structure; at about seven, words are often missed out and there is repetition because few children re-read or revise. Far more significant she believes, is phrase structure which gives a clearer indication of linguistic development. There is some evidence that the avoidance of certain constructions in writing is a consequence of immaturity as a writer rather than of chronological age. (Shaughnessy, 1977).

In his study of writing in the junior age range, Harpin (1976) found that when composing stories, young children preferred to write in the third person; at nine they had changed to writing in the first person. By contrast, most young children when attempting to write in a factual style, used the subjective, changing at nine or ten years to 'he', 'she' or 'it'. The inappropriate use of 'me' in early writing has also been noted by other researchers. (Kroll *et al*, 1980; Burgess *et al*, 1973). Another typical feature of first writing occurs in relation to verb phrases where children do not always maintain agreement between tenses in successive phrases. The greatest difficulty seems to be the selection of the correct tense for hypothetical reference and cognitively this appears to be a very late development. The narrative style of first writing is sustained by the wide use of 'and' in the main clause co-ordination. Although it supports chronological progression and the easy connection of ideas, it loses out on logicality. This is particularly evident in the instances of confusion which occur when a complex sentence is attempted. The competent use of a range of adverbial clauses is, argues Perera (1984), a clear sign of cognitive growth. Adverbial clauses of time are common in narrative, which is organised sequentially, but the introduction of a variety of clause types is a feature of the writing of older, abler pupils.

Content

For many children, there remains the problem of working out what to write, as well as how to write it. It is important therefore, not to see maturity in writing only in terms of the child's growing ability to handle complex constructions successfully. Evaluation of linguistic features needs to encompass the writers' purposes, and hence their capacity to express meaning effectively. In moving towards competence, children are unlikely to perform equally well over a range of writing tasks and mistakes will probably occur when they begin to experiment with new structures. Where written language has no oral counterpart, as for example in scientific writing, they cannot be expected to know intuitively how to produce it. A considerable intellectual challenge is posed in coping with conceptually demanding topics and new forms of knowledge simultaneously. Providing models of non-fiction writing is vital, and regular use of all sources of reference has to be encouraged.

Summary

It has been argued, that throughout the primary school years there is sequential growth in children's writing and that this appears to parallel cognitive development. Growth in skills and understanding in writing also draws substantially on social, emotional and moral development, reflecting progress from a preoccupation with self to an awareness of others and to a sharper understanding of the world and reality. This has implications for the way in which we analyse and assess children's writing, for as Wilkinson concludes, we are given:

> . . . examples of how it is possible to describe the written composition of writers of ages seven, ten and thirteen in terms not only of its style but also of its 'psychological content', by which we mean the quality of thinking, the quality of feeling, and the nature of the moral attitude displayed.
>
> (Wilkinson, 1986, p. 22)

In drawing on the Crediton model and its underlying concepts and relating this to alternative schema and classifications which emphasise general trends, some tentative assumptions have been made. This particularly so in the light of increasing evidence of patterns and sequences in the acquisition of writing skills which support a theory of developmental progression. The model outlined below is intended to support the broad analysis of children's writing, and to offer scope for assessing the individual writer and writing development.

Characteristics of stages of development in children's writing

Beginning writing

> Random writing comprising a string/chain of events, with no shape or sequence,
> Corresponds to talk,
> Use of familiar story phrases,
> Events occur within a day,
> No discussion of, explanation for actions,
> Familiar context,
> Confusion of tenses.

Ordered recording

> Coherent narrative, but minimal description,
> Sequencing of events,
> No development of events or ideas,
> No imaginative, emotive unity,
> Limited organisation of material,
> Familiar context, known people.

Beginning of organisation

> Coherent narrative account, complexity of plot increases but the whole lacks consistency,
> Beginning of characterisation and the personalising of inanimate objects,
> Some recognition of a reader,
> Some consideration of casual relationships and outcomes,
> Long introductions, little development of theme or topic,
> Familiar context, known people,

Experimenting with literary effects

> Extended composition, striving for effects, but not a unified whole,

No sustained emotional or imaginative movement,

Elaborations, modifications in deference to a reader,

Variation in scene, time and distance,

Elements of abstraction and conjecture,

More vitality and action, beginning of description,

Suggestion of atmosphere through introduction of sights and sounds,

Excessive use of dialogue,

Suggestion of moral issues, distinctions drawn between good and bad,

The beginnings of characterisation.

Self-awareness

Fully realised and satisfying narratives,

Insufficient information in non-narrative writing for complete understanding,

Coherent, spare accounts,

Some difficulties in objectivity,

Some reflective ability, self-awareness,

Development of imaginative content and of expressive elements,

Balance between narrative and dialogue,

Fuller characterisation,

Use of well-known idioms, colloquial language,

Extended vocabulary,

Evidence of global planning, endings less abrupt, accounts successfully concluded.

Elaboration and explanation

Clear, coherent, satisfying texts,

Feelings explored and examined, recognition of the actions and behaviour of others,

Competent use of different registers,

Knowledge of different conventions in writing,

Introduction of aggressive, argumentative incidents,

Adequate explanations and precisely defined terms in factual writing,

Objectivity well established, less subjective emotional involvement,

Evidence of sensitivity, impact of reading,

Extended perspectives.

CHAPTER 3

Development and Extension in Writing

In many primary classrooms, development and extension in children's writing is seen largely in terms of the acquisition of a neat script and the basics of spelling, and in the ability to construct a reasonable story or to reproduce notes or information. These are, of course, valuable skills and need to be learned if children are to be able to take advantage of the processes of schooling. But too often, writing is taught in isolation and without a supporting contextual framework to give it meaning, purpose and relevance.

Promoting a model of writing development which emphasises the links between writing and personal development has significant consequences for the nature and purpose of writing activity in the primary school. Crucially, it demands a shift in emphasis from a narrowly prescriptive view of writing as a skill learned and applied chiefly in school. Hall has observed that:

> ... the myth persists that children do not know anything about writing until they are taught it at school.
>
> (Hall, 1987, p. 41)

In drawing on current research and recent developments in the study of written language it offers a substantive basis on which to build a writing curriculum. There are three major considerations:

- The purposes for writing need to be clearly stated and understood,
- Schools and teachers need to foster the conditions in which writing will flourish and be encouraged,
- Activities and experiences have to be appropriate for the

stage of development and, ideally, ought to try to capitalise on periods of optimum interest, capability and involvement.

The purposes of writing

In the early years in school, between the ages of four and seven, children write to find out about writing. It is a time for trial, error and experiment, an opportunity to explore the possibilities and potential of writing within a stimulating and positive atmosphere.

During the transition period, usually between seven and nine years, children write to learn the conventions of writing – how to compose sentences, acquire strategies for learning to spell, the skills of handwriting, for example. At this stage the purpose of writing activity is to ensure that basic skills are learned, practised, and applied in writing across the curriculum.

In the junior years, between nine and eleven, and beyond, children write to find a voice, exploring written language as a medium for self-expression. The purpose of writing is to give confidence in what is written and how it is written. This in turn supports development in oral language.

The conditions for writing

The child

In establishing a context for writing the child's aims are more important than the teacher's. Peters (1985) argues that the stimulus for writing has to come from within the child, and Arnold (in Raban, 1985) refers to the 'will to write'. Too often in the classroom it is assumed that all children can and will write, thus ignoring the fact that for some children it may often be difficult to find something to say in writing; for others, difficult to find the words to express what they wish to say. Being able to make choices about when, how and what to write is therefore important, especially in the stages of emergent writing, when there needs to be every opportunity for fostering the child's confidence in experimenting with language.

The teacher

Giving children choices in the classroom may mean a reappraisal of the teacher's role. The Cox Report advocates an 'apprenticeship' approach in which the adult represents the 'success' the child seeks and yet offers endless help. This is precisely the relationship which exists between parent and child and which is so successful in the acquisition of speech. In the classroom such an approach could be significant in terms of the attitudes to writing that are conveyed, and the expectations that are engendered.

If teachers are to effectively avoid closing down options, they have to recognise the importance of the context in which writing occurs. Children engage in talk because its purpose and function is clear to them; the same, ideally, should be true for writing. On entry to school, it is imperative that the child is not disconnected from the literacy support systems already established in the home. Disruption is less likely to occur where the teacher can maintain the reciprocity of parent/child relationships, be guided by intuition in making responses and can offer constant feedback. Acting as a model, the teacher is seen to be a writer, providing realistic opportunities for writing, alerting children to possible choices, and stimulating interest in a variety of written responses.

The classroom

The physical arrangement of the classroom, the visual impact, the quality, range and organisation of resources, and the level of display and general presentation combine to give an impression of the variety of teaching and learning that is taking place. The priority that is given to achieving breadth and balance in the curriculum and to providing a rich and stimulating environment will be evident. Where writing is given prominence in the classroom, it is apparent that children still have access to the 'print world' that surrounds them in the community and on which their first notions of literacy are based. To complement the supply of books, both fiction and non-fiction, there will be collections of magazines, catalogues, timetables, directories and newspapers, for example. In addition, the opportunity would be found to include some or all of the following on a regular basis:

- Examples of high quality labelling. The teacher's own writing serves as a model on pegs, drawers, and cupboards, for example.
- In infant classrooms, white or black boards at the children's height, with markers or chalk available.
- A writing area, with a range of writing implements, pencils,

crayons, biros, felt tips etc.; different types and sizes of paper; note pads; envelopes; exercise books both lined and unlined. Perhaps a typewriter, tape recorder, word processor, or telephone.

- Magazines, newspapers, comics in the home-corner; pads and pencils in the shop; large sheets of paper and pencils accompanying constructional apparatus; pad and pencils beside scientific experiments and equipment.
- A display of samples of different scripts and print styles including examples of calligraphy, lettering, signs and symbols.
- An area for the display of a range of packaging, food labelling, product advertising; posters etc.
- A resource area containing telephone directories, time-tables, recipe books, calendars, diaries, journals, maps and manuals.

Component skills

It is of crucial important that schools have a policy for handwriting so that a consistent model is provided and there is continuity in objectives. Peters (1967) has shown a correlation between speed and fluency in handwriting and the quality of writing. A strong argument can be made for introducing the cursive style from the outset; children

I.4.

Where do I line up who are my freinds who are my enemyfs. I follow the rest of the class who seem to know every thing I go In to a Big room full of taBles what would the work Be like there were some nice people But whure they nice in feeling I was trembling they were all older than me. Where were all my other freinds were they feeling the same as me the teacher came in called mrs juille she had grey hair and a pretty Dress. She started talking eventually she said It was playtime and I found lots of new freinds.
The
END.

have few problems in transferring from continuous patterns to words. Marion Richardson in the 1920s and 1930s noted that print script did not lead naturally to a cursive hand, but introducing and practising continuous patterns based on letter shapes appears to give rhythm and flow which can be transferred to words and sentences in first writing. An early ease and fluency with a basic script can free a child's concentration to attend to the composing aspects of writing.

At the pre-writing stage there should be the opportunity to draw and to make patterns in a variety of media to develop fine motor control skills and to give confidence in all kinds of mark making and in handling implements. At this stage children are being encouraged to communicate through drawing, to pay attention to detail in observing and recording and in the selecting, shaping and reorganising of experiences. This can be related to writing words, phrases or sentences, but is likely to be more productively used as the basis for oral stories and accounts.

Play writing in particular should be encouraged; that is, the child's own 'writing' whether or not it resembles conventional writing. It is also valuable to encourage the 'reading' of the 'play writing'. Its importance is confirmed in the Cox Report (p. 51, 10.25) where it recommends that children 'make their own versions of things like labels, captions, lists, notices, letters and illustrated books.' Children bring to school a knowledge of print from a variety of sources – becoming literate is a developmental process which begins long before they reach school. The first stage in learning to write is a recognition that speech has a written equivalent. This recognition activates the process of identifying and learning the symbolic representations of sounds and words, the letters of the alphabet. Simultaneously, the process of translating those symbols is going on, leading to the integration of visual, auditory and tactile skills.

Virtually all activities and experiences in the infant classroom contribute to this integration and a child's understanding of the world is revealed in talk and in mark making. Creative activities (drawing, painting, model-making) are therefore useful pointers to the stage of development reached. The maximum opportunities for developing all kinds of visual communication is crucial – there is no need for formal writing lessons as such and too much reliance on paper and pencil only should be avoided.

The beginnings of handwriting

Before coming to school some children will know the names of letters, some will know the sounds, others will know both. There will also be a number who have no knowledge of letters at all. Some will be able to write a few, or even all the lower case letters of the alphabet, while others may have learned to write using only upper case letters. All of this is valuable and will form the basis of the formal teaching of the component skills of handwriting. The first step is to assess the child's existing knowledge and to build on it constructively, drawing on as wide a range of activities as possible.

Letter and word recognition

Productive use can be made of food packets, of packaging, labelling and advertising generally. Children are quite familiar with an extensive range of products and can be encouraged to look for patterns and similarities in words. It is possible to build up a useful sight vocabulary in this way, and though the words may not appear in a typical reading scheme they can be a more general resource in writing. The activity is essentially creative, the children drawing on the patterns and shapes in their own way in a variety of media. (This is the stage which corresponds to Level 1 of the statements of attainments for handwriting in the National Curriculum p. 51, 10.23)

Pattern making and letter formation

Individual letters can be practised in 2 and 3 dimensions, but at the same time, continuous patterns will also be practised to lay the foundations for cursive writing. For this kind of activity, samples of different types of print need to be available, and the children encouraged to trace, copy, draw and paint, using crayons, felt tips, paints etc. Letters and words can be made using plasticine, pebbles, twigs, pasta, etc., which on completion may be used as the basis for learning simple printing techniques.

The alphabet

Learning the names and sounds of all the lower case and capital letters will be a continuing process in the course of these activities. It can be developed in a more formal way by asking the children to

● write all the letters you know
● write all the words you know

and by practising the movements for correct letter formation. Attention will need to be paid to ensuring the correct hold of a pencil, so that the child is comfortable with the writing implement, taking the particular needs of left-handed children into account.

Procedures to be followed will include:

● Finger tracing, either in the air or on paper, to establish starting points, and to develop a fluent movement.
● Repeating the exercise with a pencil, and practising for ease and fluency.
● Tracing over pre-drawn letters.
● Free copying of examples.
● Producing the letter without a written example, when the letter name or sound is given.
● Practising combinations of letters, and then progressing to words.

The procedures are appropriate for both print and cursive script but it must be remembered that when cursive script is to be introduced, each letter will need to be formed with the necessary 'hooks' for linking to other letters. It is common practice to use only unlined paper at this stage and until children have begun to consciously attend to spacing and directionality. For some children, lines may be helpful and widely-spaced, lined paper, ought to be available.

The techniques of handwriting

The use of lined paper in learning to write legibly is perhaps implied in the Level 2 Attainment Targets in Handwriting, (p. 51, 10.23). Children are expected to produce legible upper and lower case letters with consistency, and using ascenders and descenders clearly. The value of lined paper, especially the traditional four-line practice type, in helping children to distinguish between lower and upper case letters, and in relating the proportions of letters one to another, cannot be over-emphasised. It may also help children to gradually reduce and control the size of their writing until it begins to correspond to conventionally acceptable size.

N.B. If lined paper is to be introduced from the early years, it is important that the school determines the size of line space appropriate to the stage of development, and that this is consistent with the lines in corresponding exercise books.

Handwriting exercises can be productively linked to creative activity as, for example, in the writing of a favourite poem or story, which may be mounted and illustrated. It is also vital that, from time to time, handwriting is assessed on its own merits. In later stages this does not unduly penalise the child who has difficulty in finding the content for writing. By the time the child has begun to produce a clear and legible cursive style, (Level 3 Attainment Target, p. 51, 10.23), there will have been practice in writing independent sentences, in writing simple stories, and of copying from a wide range of sources. Only if the writing that is produced is effectively linked to reading will the purpose of writing be clear, and by implication, the need for legibility. Ideally therefore, practice will also cover the making of lists and labels, the sending of messages, instructions and notes, for example, in an appropriate context.

The art of handwriting

Handwriting can become a means of artistic expression and we have only to look at the supreme achievements of calligraphers in the Islamic tradition, to be aware of its potential. In stimulating awareness of the artistic possibilities in handwriting, we may also develop children's aesthetic sensitivities. Handwriting practice therefore continues throughout the primary school, with children moving towards the development of a personal and aesthetically satisfying individual style, and to a wider concern for presentation as a whole.

Interest in all kinds of writing can again be fostered through reference to advertisements, posters, book covers, package design and labelling. An introduction to italic and copperplate writing, to Arabic scripts and Oriental characters, and to illuminated manuscripts may also provide the stimulus for creative activities which support the development of different skills and techniques. These are, in turn, applied with increasing confidence and control to everyday writing.

The use of ink pens adds a further dimension to writing development. There is usually an intensive period of adjustment on moving from the use of pencil to the use of an ink pen, but few children will find the transition too demanding. Care needs to be taken in setting reasonable expectations in the initial changeover period. Coping with writing in a new medium may mean that, for a time, children will less consciously attend to content and presentation for example, and some decline in performance is to be expected.

Fewer problems are likely to occur where efforts and energies are channelled through a combination of formal practice and creative activity.

When children are able to write independently at some length, without undue concern for the smooth flow of their handwriting, and with a clear, legible print or cursive style they should be encouraged to re-draft work and to present a fair copy. The product is now becoming as important as the process. The making of anthologies, of books for younger children, the writing of letters and the making of posters and advertisements will all give practice in publishing writing which has to meet certain criteria for presentation.

The teacher is a major influence on the quality and standard of handwriting achieved in the classroom and the level of attention to the overall presentation of writing in the classroom will affect the children's perceptions of what is expected and what can be attained. The writing curriculum ought to include the teaching of the following:

- How to set work out on the page and produce an attractive layout.
- The use of margins and their width in proportion to each other and to the amount of written text.
- The setting out of the title in relation to the text.
- The size of letters for titles and headings.
- Paragraph indentations. The use of decoration within and bordering the text.

There are obvious correlations between this sort of activity and those of drawing, painting, collage and printing, but there are also wider cross-curricular links. There are possible applications in Geography, History, R.E. and Science where the skills can be co-ordinated, for example, in keeping journals, in preparing historical documents, in map-making, in trying to write the languages of other countries and in the general presentation of information.

Legibility is fundamental to writing, and the development of well-formed handwriting must remain a central concern when we consider how much time in school is actually spent on writing tasks.

Vocabulary and spelling

Although spelling lists and spelling tests are typical of primary class-rooms, they are not always part of a structured approach to the teaching of spelling. At best, word lists may relate to the prevailing topic and are being used in context; but where spelling lists are produced, the choice of words is often based on arbitrary notions of 'match' to the children's abilities. Testing is invariably done in isolation so that children do not get any immediate opportunity to experiment with newly-learned words in a relevant task. Much of the marking and assessment of writing refers to competency in spelling in the belief that spelling is a crucial element in the clarification of meaning. The systematic acquisition of a sight vocabulary underpins writing in two crucial ways:

- it provides the words for writing
- it offers strategies for learning to spell.

As with handwriting, it is very important that there is a school policy for spelling, not a succession of word lists of increasing complexity and difficulty, but a policy which emphasies the fun of words. It should focus on the cultivation of an interest in words, in their patterns, shapes and similarities, so that children are being encouraged to devise their own strategies for spelling. It draws its dynamism from the strengths and enthusiasm of the teacher. As Peters observes,

> There is no question that the behaviour of the teacher determines more than any other single factor, whether a child does or does not learn to spell.
>
> (Peters, 1975, p. 7)

In the early years in school the child will be learning words for both reading and writing but the words that are needed for writing are not necessarily those which occur in reading schemes. Because children's first writing stems from domestic activity, they need the chance to draw on pre-school language experiences. There is a strong possibility that some children have a limited sight vocabulary of words from their immediate home community. These words can form the basis of developmental writing. On entry to school, it is clear that children do not speak in sentences, but conduct quite logical conversations, as Tough (1985) and Willes (1983) have shown in their transcripts of young children's talk. It would therefore seem inappropriate to expect young children to compose sentences at the stage of developmental writing. Kress, (1982) points out that small children equate a sentence with a line of writing. From the outset we should be developing a sensitivity to words, rather than pressing for sentences and stories.

Specific strategies

A first step might be to ask children to list all the words they know, about

- breakfast time
- being out in the car
- walking in the street
- my toys and pets.

These words may then form the basis of a spelling list, which is entirely relevant to the children's interests and experience. The teacher can then begin the more systematic development of strategies for spelling, which can be productively related to writing practice.

e.g. oo as in book, took, look;
    ee as in feel, heel, wheel.

What is essential is that the teacher should encourage a close study of words, especially in view of the findings of Peters (1970) who identified three factors which were particularly associated with success in spelling:

- verbal intelligence;
- visual perception of word form;
- carefulness.

Although there are sound reasons for the traditional practice of providing each child with a word book, in which are written the spellings the child needs, it would obviously be a more efficient use of teacher time and classroom resources to build up a class 'word bank'. This system, increasingly used in schools in which children are being encouraged towards independent learning, usually comprises a wall-mounted display of word cards, to which teacher and pupils contribute. It therefore represents the vocabulary in regular use, and the words, written on a folded card, are easily accessible. This is a useful mechanism for reducing the long queues of children waiting for help with spelling from the teacher. The children are not only involved in creating the 'bank', they are also encouraged to apply the 'look, cover, write, check' techniques as they add to it. This is a method of visual reinforcement focusing the child's attention on the look of a word. It requires the child to

- look at a word,
- cover the word,
- write the word,
- then check with the original word.

Although the procedure does take time, both to establish and to sustain, it has obvious benefits for both teacher and pupil. All children have an increasingly extensive vocabulary on which to draw, and can use other children as a source of help in selecting and recognising words. The teacher supports individual learning as and when appropriate, giving the child an opportunity to study new words more closely before using them in writing. The usual alternative is for the teacher to write words into a word book and the word is applied in writing before it has had a chance to become internalised.

Dictionaries

A policy for spelling ought to include guidelines for the introduction and use of dictionaries. In the National Curriculum Attainment Targets for Reading, Level 2 (p. 43) it is stated that pupils should be able to 'demonstrate a knowledge of the alphabet and its application (e.g. in word books, dictionaries and reference books).' Reading and spelling are mutually facilitating activities and there are wide-ranging alphabet-based games and procedures in infant classrooms which lead naturally towards simple dictionary work. Throughout the primary years these activities can be constructively developed to provide tasks of increasing complexity, involving, for instance, the use of reference books, or a thesaurus or card index system, so providing the foundations of independent learning. This would mean a progression from putting a random group of words into alphabetical order:

e.g. long, play, run, home, dog.

To putting words beginning with the same letter into order:

e.g. swim, sleep, sock, spin, shirt,

and to words in which the third or fourth letter may need to be taken into account:

e.g. crisp, cream, critic, creep, crown.

Other activities might include,

- Preparing an index for class project work which has been collected into book form; at an individual level this may be done for a journal or diary.
- Putting a selection of books into alphabetical order according to author, or classifying according to subject, as a preparation for general library studies.
- Setting tasks for older juniors which involve the use of a thesaurus. E.g. look at all the entries under 'air' as the basis of a study.

At all stages children can be encouraged to devise their own word and spelling games, using dictionaries as the starting point. It should be a matter of school policy that different sets (not necessarily one for each child) of dictionaries should be available throughout the school. More importantly, their use in all language activities has to be identified and progressively extended.

Reading books

All reading books, whether or not part of a scheme, fiction or non-fiction, are a potential source of words, and a support in spelling. This is particularly true of those books which children themselves own and refer to frequently, because they are about things that interest them. Where children are genuinely keen to learn and have identified a purpose for reading, they reveal a capacity for knowledge which may far exceed their performance in other respects. Their interest may therefore provide an important resource in terms of a specific sight vocabulary, and there should always be the maximum encouragement for children's own choice of reading.

Topic/project work

Classroom lists of words relating to topic themes are characteristic of many primary classrooms; again they may be further developed to include strategies for spelling, especially as these can be linked to tasks which require pupils to apply the words in an appropriate context. The Bullock Report (D. E. S. 1975, p. 528) stressed the need for a 'words in context' approach to spelling, and it is probably in the exploration of topic ideas and experiences that children will have the opportunity to use technical, scientific, geographical and historical terms. The kind of written tasks that are associated with projects are generally more factual than other writing activities and therefore demand different styles of writing and a more precise, deliberate use of words.

Working with words

In the upper infant/lower junior years, the listing of words suggested earlier will continue, although children will now be writing at greater length. As an alternative to the writing of news or stories, the following suggestions alert children to the careful choice of relevant vocabulary.

Prepare a shopping list for:

- making a cake,
- building a garage,
- things to take on holiday,
- party food.

The chosen list of words can be discussed by a group or by the class, and, at a later stage, be the basis of more extended writing.

Sending messages – simple instructions from teacher to pupil or from pupil to pupil, which require a brief answer. This can be part of a silent thinking activity when the emphasis is on the choice of words and the accuracy of the message.

Words to describe

- my cat,
- my best friend,
- in the garden,
- in the playground.

Words to describe emotions:

- happy, sad, lost, uncomfortable, frightened, pleased.

Fun with words can come from word games and does not exclude the use of commercial resources. Brownjohn (1982) has produced some lively and imaginative ideas which will enliven the spelling programme

A policy for spelling and vocabulary development, while supporting the formal aspects of the writing curriculum, and leading towards precision and accuracy, should not be dictated by pressures for 'correctness'. Ultimately the aim is to give pupils access to a wide choice of words, so that they are able to manipulate language with understanding, and convey meaning more accurately. It is not simply a question of introducing longer, more complicated words, into their writing. There has to be flexibility of approach so that children are not discouraged from attempting to write and spell their own words, or from resorting to blank lines where they may be unsure of a spelling. This will only occur where the teacher allows mistakes to be made and offers a strategy for coping with them.

The planning and organisation of writing

The fact that writing can be consciously planned and organised only becomes apparent to children when recognition of a reader imposes the need to be clear and explicit. A readiness to shape and refine writing is also dictated by knowledge of the purposes of writing, so that planning and organisation becomes part of a deliberate attempt to make a measured and appropriate response in writing.

Emergent writing is essentially a planning process. Early narratives are a means of exploration about what writing looks like, and crucially, what it tells the writer about their own thoughts. The process is therefore still more important than the product, and it is inappropriate and unrewarding, at this stage of development, to attempt to deal with anything other than surface features. The nature of the task, the context within which it is undertaken, the resources the individual child brings to the task will all impinge on the manner and style of the response, but notions of improving on a text are alien to younger children. Their writing represents first thoughts – it develops in front of them and is not supported or guided by a view of the whole as a finished entity. Long term planning, in the sense of having at the outset, a clear picture of what the end-product will look like, depends on the ability to retain interest in and control over the material, both cognitively and practically. This demands the manipulation of abstract information concerning time, space, people and events, and the language to express it.

Pupils in the infant classroom are mainly concerned with practising writing. Thinking about what to write is a sufficient demand. Planning as such is related to the external superficial aspects of writing, and teacher attention will concentrate on improving surface features, including size of letters, spacing of words and the organisation of the writing on the page. As far as possible it should spring from the child's own words, phrases and sentences. The organisation of first stories – usually a loose, unpunctuated piece of writing – tends to reflect the child's familiarity with the conventions of story structures. Consequently we find embedded in the narrative typical beginnings and endings, and perhaps, familiar characters. This is an important stage of development because it marks a shift from writing as speech to a story framework which, in time, will form the basis of whole-text planning. Activities to support this development might include:

- Sentence building from a selection of words.
- Describing daily activities in the order in which they occur, to establish notions of time and sequence.
- Building up stories from a group of sentences, preferably where there is no right order, but several possibilities.
- Re-ordering sentences taken from prose or poetry
- Using picture/story sequences to establish the idea of continuity. Initially stories could be based on commercial sets of pictures, but there should be progress towards the production of children's own picture and story sequences. The use of comics may provide a starting point for this activity, with strips cut into single pictures which the children have first to re-order and then read, to check if the story makes sense. The same procedures can then be applied to their own story sequences, so that they are involved in setting tasks for each other.
- Re-telling and re-writing familiar stories.
- What happens next? Predicting what might happen next in a story. This may be linked to books and stories read by the teacher, and also to the child's own reading. (It is a useful source of information about the level of the child's understanding of what is being read). This could be an individual or group activity.
- Children collaborating as a group to put a story together. Each writes a section after discussion, and then all decide how to combine their individual efforts into a whole. This activity will provide opportunities for reading, for the sharing and pooling of ideas and may be a valuable support for children who find it difficult to find ideas for writing.
- Variations on the Graves (1983) model of teacher/pupil 'conferences' can be adopted, which might include the teacher writing with the children. This is particularly important with younger children because it establishes a model for being able to conduct their own conferences, once they have the

confidence to do so. It may start quite simply as a discussion on how the story might begin, what is going to happen in the story, and how it is going to end. Gradually more formal systems for 'brain-storming' may be introduced, with an emphasis throughout on the children's contributions. A vital component of this process is that the teacher writes with the pupils, shares ideas, perhaps makes notes for reference, either on a blackboard or, when working with a smaller group, on a large sheet of paper in the middle of the table.

● Describing and recording daily activities either in the home or in school, e.g. how to clean teeth, how to make a sandwich, how to make a model or paint a picture; this can be further developed across the curriculum by linking it to scientific experiments, to technical and problem-solving activities.

● Older children can be asked to write another, or an alternative page or chapter for their reading book.

Constructive intervention in the writing process is possible after about seven years of age, though this is not to imply that younger children cannot benefit from attempts to revise or re-draft their writing. This is, however, a teacher-intensive activity, and it may be unrealistic to expect more than a fair copy. Children will tend to repeat the same mistakes because thy are more concerned with what is written than with secretarial aspects. As teachers we tend to move too quickly from marking content only, and mark 'experiments' and 'attempts' as faults rather than valuing them as efforts in mastering the medium. Wilkinson reminds us that 'organisation is crucial in writing for whatever purpose and may be exceedingly difficult to achieve'. (1986, p. 114)

For this reason it is necessary in the junior years to regularly discuss how writing can be organised. This will inevitably require the study of a range of texts and will draw on prose and poetry, fiction and non-fiction, automatically relating reading and writing activities in a purposeful and relevant context. A close study of different kinds of writing, could enable children to begin to be aware of differing styles and forms and to begin to identify their characteristics.

At this stage planning and organisation becomes an activity in its own right and children can be actively encouraged to try out their own ideas, to find different ways of preparing for writing, and to develop individual strategies for planning. The following example was produced by a boy of 9 years of age who had always been reluctant to

I do not like writing stories even if I have to
I like reading stories but I hate writing. I do not like writing stories
The End
In
more
ways than
one and thats that
The End
I hate writing stories. I will not

when
                          why
                         a joke
at breakfast   my brother   April fool
     milk and butter   giggled

                  where frogs live in
                   ponds
little   sit on lily pads
footprints   a frog in the fridge
froggy

                   keep quiet
                   nobody speaks
opened door put table not a word
everyone back
took out noticed
looked move first carefully
custard-skin there closed
left-over like sitting ignored
started laughed their

The frog in the fridge.

I opened the fridge and there he was
sitting on the skin of the left-over custard
Like it was a lily pad in a pond.
A frog in the fridge cant be ignored,
but who will move first him or me?
Me!
I took out the milk and butter
I closed the door very carefully
I put the milk on the table and everyone
started their breakfast.
No one noticed the little froggy footprints
in the butter.
I went back and opened the door and there
he was.
Still there!
Back to my breakfast.
I looked at everyone all eating like there
wasn't a frog in the fridge.
Until my brother started to giggle and
everyone laughed.
Frog in the fridge they said
April fool!

write. He produced the three pieces in succession, while working with a retired journalist who had come to school to help the older pupils with writing.

Brainstorm sessions will present an opportunity to explore topic webs, flow diagrams, lists and note-taking. Beginning to write shouldn't necessarily depend on having a total view of the finished piece in mind at the outset – making a start enables a child to organise and marshall thoughts. The help of other children can be enlisted for proof reading, and they should be encouraged to read their work to each other in order to find out if it makes sense.

Planning and organisation for the child means a chance to:

- sort out ideas and information,
- select and reject material,
- put the material into order,
- set it out to best advantage on the paper,
- gain control of surface features,
- review and re-write.

It will generate such questions as:

- who is the writing for?
- what is its purpose?
- what has to be conveyed?
- how is it to be structured?
- what is the most appropriate style?
- to what extent do presentational aspects have to be taken into account?
- how important is spelling, punctuation etc;?

Planning and organisation for the teacher means supporting the child in devising internal strategies for coping with the demands of writing. Children need to be given regular and systematic practice in the following:

- working from notes, (therefore practice in note-taking),
- posing questions which may be answered in writing; this would most readily be done in relation to topic and project work, planning for writing, individually and in groups, or with response partners,
- listing words, ideas,
- looking for and collating resources for writing before making a start; dictionaries, readers, information, texts,
- presenting information diagrammatically,
- sending messages,
- letter writing,
- scientific notes,
- poetry writing e.g. haiku.

It is crucial to remember, in the primary classroom, that adult notions of what constitutes a well-structured text may detract from evaluating writing for its aesthetic qualities, with a tendency to concentrate on mechanical skills. We must also take account of the physical context in which writing occurs, which will have a profound effect upon the child's capacity to plan and to organize. Time limits are restrictive especially as getting started may take considerable time. The freedom to ponder, plan and prepare to write requires the absence of 'artificial' writing times. Ideally we have to capitalise on and respond to children's interests and enthusiasms.

The content of writing

There ought to be clear evidence of progression in writing tasks in the primary school, with an extension of demand not only in the subject matter, but also in the form, style and presentation of material. It may be argued that story-writing in the primary school is over-exploited at the expense of other kinds of writing. The balance can be maintained by setting out a programme of writing activities which are related to stages of development and are realistically within the child's capabilities. The suggestions offered build on the child's first instincts to write about self, moving on to awareness of others in relation to self, and eventually to a capacity for objectivity and impartiality.

A possible developmental progression in writing activities and experiences:

(1) Emergent and developmental writing draws on pre-school experience, and can be channelled as follows;
   – All the words I know.
   – Interesting words I can see in the room.
   – Words I like in my reading book.
   – Words I use at home.
(2) Narrative writing from experience – home/school/holidays. To avoid repetition, and to give a sharp focus, consider titles such as:
   (a) I didn't do it!   (b) Mary's unhappy day,
   (c) The lonely child   (d) The man was angry
   (e) Who did that?   (f) Nobody likes me
(3) Keeping diaries and journals of home/school activities, as an alternative to news time, perhaps a class diary.
(4) Accounts of, or the ordering of events of school or class visits, prepared as a joint activity.
(5) The teacher reads part of a story – children discuss and write what they think will happen next, or what happened before.
(6) The children prepare a story orally, each contributing a word, idea or a sentence. The teacher then writes it out, on the

board or on a sheet of paper. It is then read aloud, removed, and the children asked to write it out as accurately as possible. It may of course be referred to by the children if necessary.

(7) Re-writing familiar stories. This helps children to sequence events.

(8) Pretend you are: a witch, a bully, an animal, a grown-up.

(9) Making lists: recipes, items needed for an experiment, for making a model, vocabulary for a topic or project. These activities will be linked to spelling and vocabulary development.

As children become more at ease with writing, and capable of periods of sustained concentration, the range of tasks can be extended to include:

(10) Writing stories for younger children and less able readers. The stories can be printed, published and taped, for use in the school library.

(11) Reports and transactional writing arising from classroom and home activities, where children have to concentrate on giving precise information in chronological order.

(12) Making notes – links especially to topic work, but includes the sequencing of class/school activities, outings and events. For juniors this would also involve the making of tables, graphs, charts, route maps etc. and relate to pictorial representation generally. It is therefore an essential element in cross-curricular work.

(13) Use of stimuli: e.g. pictures, paintings, photographs, music, literature, artefacts, and newspapar articles. They may be used to find out about things past and present, near and far; for arousing interest; or to assist in writing about the unfamiliar. Imagination, creativity and fantasy may be called for in writing about the unfamiliar, therefore discussion is very important, and strategies for self-cueing need to be established. Creativity is not something that can be taught as Arnold (1985) would argue, but teachers can provide a context in which it may flourish. The use of objects and visual stimuli should not be excluded especially where children are experiencing difficulty in coping with events, actions and people outside their usual frame of reference.

(14) Poetry writing – based on listening to and sampling a wide

range of poetry. It has to be recognised, however, that highly-charged emotional responses are more a part of the adult world than of the average child's. An understanding of the subtleties of poetic language, and the capacity to manipulate imagery, metaphor and symbolism only comes with intellectual maturity. Rhymes, verse and songs provide an introduction to the form. The constraints imposed by the need to express ideas succinctly and precisely may act as a spur to effort, but not all children will find a voice in poetry. There needs to be full and frequent discussion of poetry if it is to make sense to children and the teacher's enthusiasm is the catalyst for their responses.

(15) Imagine you are: a politician
　　　　　　　　　 a journalist
　　　　　　　　　 an explorer
　　　　　　　　　 an entertainer.

Writing of this kind will be prefaced by discussion, either whole class or in groups, when differing viewpoints and perspectives will form the basis of discussion so that the end products reflect a range of responses according to individual interpretation.

(16) Recall of incidents:
　　　　 (a) when I was happy, surprised, glad,
　　　　 (b) when I was sad, embarrassed, shocked.

(17) Letter writing: informal to family, friends; formal to thank, to request information, to give information. This will provide an opportunity to engage in writing for a 'real' purpose, and will have obvious cross-curricular relevance. Children can for example, be encouraged to write to shops, firms, parents, companies, M.P.s, and others, offering ideas and suggestions or asking for information.

(18) To develop sensitivity – writing from different perspectives, and exploring different reactions within a given situation. This could be based on a newspaper or television report, or a book.

(19) Telephone conversations which are initially set up orally. They may be based on interactions between two particular people in imaginary or real situations. The context will be one in which the child has to adopt a different character. E.g. as a customer making a complaint.

(20) Writing at length – introduce the idea of chapters, episodes and continuing adventures.

(21) Introduce elements of technical writing. Describing experiments; using geographical terms; writing arising from problem solving and mathematical activities; writing necessary in craft, design and technology. This will give a chance to consider different forms of presentation and style in writing tasks.

(22) Planning and writing advertisements, jingles and television commercials.

(23) Persuasive writing to convince a reader. Link to and develop from current affairs and topic work. Avoid too obviously controversial subjects and well-rehearsed public 'issues'. Deal with children's own stated concerns and experiences from which they can begin to generalise.

(24) Responding to a wide range of literary sources, not only modern 'children's writers'. Attempting to write in the style of a particular author. This will be related to the reading programme and children will require a good working knowledge of a range of authors and their fiction. It will involve the examination and discussion of texts as process as well as products; how the story has been constructed; what makes one author distinctly different from another; how effects are achieved? Sharing books is a contributory factor in writing development.

(25) Writing about ordinary, everyday events in a sensational or humorous style, perhaps as a journalist.

(26) Précis or summary – a skill to be taught. Underline important words and phrases, or re-process the information under headings or in tabulated form. (D. A. R. T. S. – Directed Activities Related to Texts procedures – are relevant here).

(27) Play writing – plays need to be read first to establish the format. A start can be made by re-writing folk or fairy tales in play form. The whole class may participate in writing a serial for example.

(28) Critical review of books, fact and fiction, television programmes, plays, comics, newspapers and magazines. Discuss issues of bias.

(29) Devise rhymes, limericks, riddles and jokes. Publish the products.

(30) After debate and discussion – sum up different points of view and express an opinion.

(31) Make use of printers wherever appropriate, and especially where work is to be published for a wider audience.

(32) Making notes, a practice which should begin at the infant stages, and be continuously developed.

Inevitably, because children do not work or progress at the same rate and bring differing capabilities to the tasks, not all children will successfully master all of these skills in writing. Most of the suggested activities will need to be regularly practised and refined throughout the primary years. It is therefore vital that a language policy adopts a cross-curricular approach to writing, and that writing permeates the curriculum. The ideal, as Smith concludes, is that:

> Writing develops as an individaul develops, in many directions, continually, usually, inconspicuously, but occasionally in dramatic and unforeseeable spurts. And, like individual human development, writing requires nourishment and encouragement rather than a restraining regimen.
>
> (Smith, 1982, p. 203)

Pupils will be encouraged to write where there is the opportunity for:

- games to be invented,
- rules to be written,
- songs to be sung,
- plays to be acted,
- books to be published,
- information to be stored,
- facts to be found,
- letters to be written,
- radio/television programmes to be analysed, criticised,
- reports to be prepared,
- advertisements to be displayed,
- opinions to be sought,
- surveys to be conducted,
- complaints to be aired,
- evidence to be weighed,
- judgements to be made,
- protests to be launched,
- ideas to be shared,
- worlds to be constructed,

- places to be seen, areas to be explored,
- paintings to be appreciated,
- artefacts to be studied,

as well as stories to be told. Writing will occur in conjunction with singing, painting, dancing, acting, problem-solving and building with bricks. Where the context is specific the content is likely to be strong, and the activities themselves will present a range of options rather than one set response. Real understanding, and interest, comes not from class text books on aspects of grammar or comprehension, but from the children's own investigations, where they pose the questions, seek out the answers and decide how to present the information. Investigations can arise in history, geography, science, music and R.E. for example.

A topic or project can, of course, provide cohesion, particularly in the various skills it demands. Well-conceived, it can present realistic and relevant challenges in personal, social and cognitive learning. It is a fruitful method of responding to differing abilities in writing, and for exploiting individual gifts and potential. Other possibilities include:

- Asking children to plan and prepare a talk on their hobbies or interests. It will need to contain detailed and specific information.
- Drawing attention to language used in certain contexts, e.g. P.E., music, mathematics, and discuss the characteristics of words peculiar to these areas; produce a glossary of terms.
- Setting up problem-solving activities and encouraging children to devise their own.
- Preparing guide books, travel brochures, phrase books, scientific journals, recipe books, technical manuals, a book of beliefs, for example.
- In local studies, talking to, interviewing people. Inviting them into school to talk so that children have an opportunity to make notes.
- Conducting surveys in class, in school, in the community as for example, in the Domesday project.
- Planning and mounting exhibitions, which involves making posters, labels, notices and brochures.

Cohesion and coherence

Producing a clear, fluent and intelligible piece of writing which has a sense of unity implies

- a synthesis of the component skills
- an ability to focus on the forms and patterns of language itself,
- a deliberate shaping of the text.

Bereiter (1980) emphasises that writing development may involve sucessively discrete forms of cognitive organisation, and that making one stage automatic greatly facilitates progress to the next stage. He concludes that two conditions must obtain for full integration: 'automization' and 'highly skilled time-sharing.'

In making judgements about writing at this level, we are no longer concerned with surface features (though these will contribute to the general clarity of the text, and punctuation is an issue), but with the overall impression the writing creates. We are also necessarily concerned with the significance it has for the writer and the cognitive gains that have been made. If we accept Donaldson's (1978) belief, that schooling, with its decontextualised routines and procedures, enables children to learn to cope with the world in abstract terms, then we ought to be seeing evidence of this in their writing. To support children in the development of writing in terms of cohesion and coherence, teachers will have to consciously and progressively foster an inclination to:

- recreate an experience in language,
- describe an experience, event or activity, accurately and precisely,
- write vividly and originally,
- discuss the organisation of their writing,
- use stylistic devices,
- revise and re-draft their work,
- be clear about meaning and intentions.

Framing questions about children's writing, (e.g. is it interesting, satisfying?) may illuminate for teachers some of the difficulties of composing.

As Emig (1981) reminds us, there is a danger that we 'underconceptualise and oversimplify the process'. It is therefore useful to seek children's views on what writers need to be able to do to write well, and by gaining insight into the nature of their concepts of writing, we can begin to intervene constructively in the process and set appropriate aims and objectives. To pay equal attention to all the things that must be dealt with simultaneously in writing is not realistic and achieving synthesis could be dependent upon responses in terms of feeling and effect. In making a conscious effort, in the desire for a personal voice, cognitive potential can be released in the search for meaning and self-knowledge. At issue is what Bruner (1975) describes as 'analytic competence' and which Wilkinson asserts is fundamental in education. It is the power of thinking and feeling, and the capacity for reflection. In the Cox Report it states that:

> For the individual author, writing can have cognitive functions in clarifying and supporting thought. (Spoken language also allows thoughts to be formulated in one's own words, but written language has the added advantage of making a detached reflection on them possible.) Such writing is essentially private.
>
> (Cox Report, DES 1988 p. 46, 10.5)

This confirms Wilkinson's belief in personal growth through writing as a communicative and psychological process. Cohesion in writing is achieved once difficult cognitive processes have become internalised and unconscious, and the writer can begin to implement choices. When the choices have been made the writer is then able to '. . . exercise greater control, establish ownership, and with ownership, pride and satisfaction'. (Graves, 1983, p. 21)

Nevertheless, quality in children's writing cannot be achieved by practice alone – the teacher has to provide models of writing to which pupils can begin to approximate. Smith (1983) stresses that 'reading is the only sufficiently rich and reliable source of information'. In their plea for a wider use of literature in schools, Hutchcroft *et al.* (1981) argue that 'We think it is perilous for schools to ignore the education of children's emotions.' The potential for enriching the life of classrooms that comes from literature, and the creative arts generally, is well documented. It is the means by which children come to know their own inner world of images, ideas and fantasies, it acts as a catalyst in releasing and transforming the emotions, it enriches the memory and provides an endless source of knowledge and excitement through which the imagination is nourished. It heightens and intensifies the real world. For Vandell the impact of children's literature

> . . . lies in its power to elicit emotion and empathy . . . because literature is a passionate presentation rather than an

abstraction of formal reasoning, it helps the reader (adult or child) to realise what human emotions are and the range of these emotions.

(Vandell, 1987, pp. 2,3)

Schooling provides many opportunities for children to write in the language of their immediate linguistic environment, and many of the writing tasks they undertake do no more than reinforce what they already know. Listening to, sharing and reading stories and poetry, including that drawn from other countries, is a means of extending the range of linguistic experience and of developing a sensitivity to other cultural perspectives.

In the early stages of writing, stories have an important function in the development of narrative. As children become more accomplished writers, they begin to test out stylistic devices in an attempt to improve the expressive quality of their writing. Although this may at first appear contrived and artificial, it indicates a significant phase in cognitive development, marking a deliberate effort by the writer to manipulate language which is not yet part of oral speech. It introduces a new dimension to writing – awareness of form. Graves (1983) suggests that the secret is to surround children with literature. This implies the need for a school policy for literature and the personal commitment and enthusiasm of individual teachers. The policy would need to relate to issues of aesthetic sensitivity, discernment, curiosity, enthusiasm and understanding, and be founded on the intrinsic pleasure and enjoyment that comes from books.

A school literature policy

This should address the needs of teachers and pupils and also take account of the school and classroom context. The Cox Report, makes the following recommendations of a general nature.

The environment provided by the school should promote the reading development of all pupils. Examples of purposeful and pleasurable uses of print should be displayed in classrooms, foyers and school libraries. Well chosen picture books, poetry collections, folk tales, stories, novels, reference books and non-fiction should be available for use in all primary classrooms. Well presented notices, labels and children's own work should also be displayed to stress the communicative character of the written word.

(Cox Report, DES 1988, p. 41, 9.8)

In addition consideration would also be given to the following:

- A school bookshop, book club, a book week or book events.
- Opportunities to invite authors, poets, journalists to visit the school, perhaps even to have one 'in residence'. Local firms can sometimes be persuaded to sponsor this type of activity.
- Assemblies provide a focus for parents as readers, and for the introduction of rare or unusual books. A large family Bible could generate a wide-ranging historical, geographical and sociological study, or an interest in changing fashions in names.
- The systematic development of library skills; whole class library sessions for research, browsing and choosing.
- Recommended reading lists, prominently displayed in the school, to which teachers, parents and pupils contribute.
- A workshop for the making and publishing of the school's own books. It may involve collaboration between teachers and parents, the use of printers and other technical aids.

The classroom

A comfortable, attractive book area or corner, can be created, to be used as an integral part of teaching and learning. It will be central to reading and writing activity and the books are there to serve as a stimulus, as models and as a support system. Depending on the age of the children, the selection could include:

> picture books, myths and legends, folk tales, nursery rhymes, poetry and verse, stories from other countries and in other languages, songbooks, hymn books, plays, modern children's literature, classical books, biographies, and a full range of reference books. It may be that not all books are in the book corner at the same time – it is refreshing to be able to vary the selection from time to time. The choice will vary according to work, topics or themes in progress.

The teacher

The teacher has the important task of providing rewarding literary experiences, for enhancing the child's capacities for writing, and for reading with increasing perception and reflection. It is therefore important to be seen as someone who owns and uses books, and who is willing to share and discuss all types of books. It is valuable, even with infant children, to talk with them about the criteria for choosing books, and to encourage critical judgements about books.

Hutchcroft (1981) provides the following reasons for the inclusion of literature in the primary school:

Literature:

- as stories and poems: the power of narrative and the impact on reading
- in learning: the development of patterns and structures of thought and of language to express them
- for empathy: the process of de-centring, developing sympathy
- as confirmation of personal experience: the process of finding one's place in the world
- for emotional experience: learning to explore, express and control the emotions
- for pleasure.

In offering a wide range of literary resources, the authors propose that the gains that are made are consistent with a view of 'literature for life'. They reaffirm the conclusions of the Bullock Report that 'literature shapes the personality, refines the sensibility and sharpens the critical intelligence.'

CHAPTER 4

Responding to children's writing

The study of development in children's writing within the wider context of personal development has important consequences for classroom practice, for the role of the teacher, and particularly for the ways in which the teacher responds to writing. The teacher creates the context and purpose for writing and is the main audience for that writing. In becoming writers, pupils do need to know that what they write will be received and valued; so that the manner and style of the teacher's response will have crucial long-term implications in relation to children's attitudes and commitment to writing. Where teachers consciously create an atmosphere in which what is unique and personal to the child is given a place and a voice, the response to the writing that is produced has to be both sensitive and intimate if it is to carry conviction.

It is of course, much more difficult to quantify feelings than it is to note inconsistencies in spelling. If teachers are to make a genuine response to children's writing and to monitor progress effectively, looking for evidence of personal growth as well as technical competence, then a natural concern with objective standards of correctness has to be balanced by subjective judgements. This involves not only knowing how and when to respond to a range of different types of writing, but will, on occasions, include the interpretion of an individual construction of meaning. In this context, what is an appropriate response and how is it conveyed to the child? Clearly, a mark or grade would have little significance when what is needed is confirmation or reassurance that the intended meaning has been communicated.

Marking or responding?

The impact of the teacher as the reader of children's writing has been stressed by Smith (1983) particularly in relation to the marking of writing. It is obvious that we need to go beyond the surface and linguistic features, those aspects of writing which can be readily "marked", and consider other, perhaps more qualitative criteria. A clear distinction needs to be drawn between marking, which sets out to inspect writing for flaws and errors, and responding, which seeks to support the child's efforts in the search for meaning. Fundamental to this perspective is the quality of the pupil/teacher relationship and the context in which it is sustained. It is an approach based on mutual confidence and trust, which applauds the process of writing and does not insist on what Hutchcroft (1981) calls, 'first-time perfection.'

Nevertheless, one of the anomalies of school-life is the emphasis that children themselves put on the marking of their work, and it is not always easy to persuade pupils that other kinds of responses are equally valid. It is certainly true, as Peel has observed, that:

> At all stages children must know and feel that what they write is respected by the teacher. They are proud of their work and need the recognition of some form of marking.
>
> (Peel, 1967, p. 165)

The practice of showing all work to the teacher is soon established, and marking provides the seal of approval on tasks completed, a verdict on the end-product, which makes no reference to the overall process of composing and writing. The danger is that marking becomes an end in itself, and pupils over-concerned with 'correctness'. Dunsbee and Ford also comment on the effect of marking out of ten, claiming that it leads to,

> The bad habit of expecting a mark for everything written, so that marks become more sought after than a reader's opinon.
>
> (Dunsbee and Ford 1980, p. 9)

Few primary schools now operate a policy or system which awards marks or grades for work, in the belief that they serve no useful purpose in the development and extension of skills and competencies. Not all schools have a policy for marking, though most schools have some shared principles and practices; all teachers recognise and accept that pupils value constructive comment on what has been achieved.

Praise and encouragement is often a significant part of this response, but there is also an evaluative element to it – the positive and negative effects of the teacher cannot be overlooked. A school marking policy will promote consistency of approach, and it need not exclude the personal response of individual teachers, as exemplified in the 'dialogue' which some teachers conduct with pupils, through the medium of a journal or personal log.

Once in school, pupils invariably find that their linguistic behaviour is, in Kress's (1982) words, constantly 'subject to prohibitions and injunctions.' Part of the difficulty that pupils face in learning to write in school, is that of knowing what is acceptable. Increasingly, in respect of writing, schools are moving towards the 'marking response' recommended in the Cox Report, a response that is intended to foster the pupil's confidence in experimenting with language. It is based on a belief that:

> The marking response can play a vital part in promoting this linguistic growth through establishing a dialogue and not merely concerning itself with surface features of the writing or the routine correction of technical errors.
>
> (Cox Report, 10.45, p. 54)

This response centres on support for pupils while in the act of writing, with the teacher intervening at intervals in an attempt to minimise difficulties and to maintain interest and involvement. Dialogue, between teacher and pupil and between pupils is an essential feature of the approach, in which writing becomes a joint activity, a partnership, with a sharing of ideas and advice.

Intervention

The notion of intervention in the writing process has been extensively explored by Bereiter and Scardamalia (1982), who argue that such strategies can enable pupils to produce more structural elements – reasons, examples and elaborations, for instance. By contriving a situation or context in which pupils feel comfortable and unconstrained, the teacher can prompt and guide without imposing on the style or content of the writing. Intervention is not guaranteed to improve the overall quality of writing, but it does enable pupils to devise their own supportive strategies. The ability to self-cue, for example, is important for development; evaluating writing sentence by sentence may help the pupil to retain an overall plan of the text; concentration can be improved, especially where pupils work in pairs, and attention is focused on the composing process.

The teacher/pupil conference recommended by Graves (1983), and already well-documented, has been influential in directing teachers' attention to the writing process. He was concerned that pupils were not experiencing writing as a process of trial and error, involving the drafting, revising, selecting and discarding of material until a text is satisfying. He believes that teachers themselves need to be engaged, with the pupils, in the act of writing. Not only will this provide a model for pupils, it will serve a diagnostic function for the teacher, who could gain insight into the nature of children's concepts about writing. The object of the conferencing procedure is to produce a 'publishable' piece of writing which is generated by an initial brainstorming session, followed by writing, during which the teacher moves around, either checking progress or conferencing with those in need. On completion, the writing, including that of the teacher, is read aloud, and comment and criticism invited.

Certain classroom procedures have to be enforced if the activity is to be worthwhile – access to spelling lists, paper and dictionaries is vital, and there should be minimal interruption once writing is under way. It does of course take time to establish the routines of conferencing, and to build up pupil confidence to a point where they genuinely seek advice from the teacher. Realistically, it will not be the only approach to writing employed, as it is difficult to sustain the initial impact, but the importance of the procedure lies in its potential to develop and enrich the teacher/pupil partnership in writing.

Responding to writing necessarily involves teachers in being explicit about their expectations of pupils, not simply in setting out the requirements of a specific task, but also in suggesting ways in which pupils might begin to tackle it, and crucially, in outlining what the product might look like. To begin to write independently, children need to have access to a range of strategies: flow diagrams, topic webs, brainstorming etc., and be free to make choices about which to adopt and how to proceed. The model of the writing process produced by the National Writing Project, demostrates how this might be done:

Aspect of writing	might involve	might look like
Starting writing	getting ideas, brain-storming, flow diagrams, discussions with a friend, group or class journals, ideas sheets, negotiating and thinking about the purpose, audience	a list, drawing, word web scribbled notes (or there might be no physical record at all)
Composing	developing the text on paper as quickly as possible, without worrying too much about spelling at this stage, gathering more information, thinking about the audience, experiment-ing with vocabulary, structure sequence, colla-borating	a continuous text legible at least to the writer
Revising	sharing and seeking a response from peers, seeking a preliminary response from the intended audience, reading it aloud or to themselves, asking, does it make sense? does it sound right? have I said what I intended?	a text with crossings out, boxes and arrows, additions, question marks, cut up and reassembled text
Editing	attending to spelling, fine details of punctuation, preparing for publication to a real audience, editing in small groups, using dictionaries	a text with corrections
Publishing	making decisions about what to publish, how to publish, where to publish, typing, neat handwriting, word processing	a clean, neat handwritten or typed text, letter, book, (or a model, lecture broadcast, play, advert.)

(National Curriculum Council, Nelson, 1989)

Though not intended as a scheme, the model does indicate that a major part of the teacher's response is to encourage pupils towards independence in writing; so that evidence of developing maturity in writing will be seen where a pupil takes increasing responsibility for writing. As a process it shows the child that the teacher values drafts and first attempts as well as polished pieces, and confirms that writing is not necessarily a solitary activity. It also promotes the setting up of 'response partners', pairs or groups of children who discuss, share, edit and evaluate each others writing. The teacher acts as a facilitator, guiding pupils towards a 'published' text, but enabling choices and decisions to be made by the children in the process.

The writing curriculum

Judgements about writing will be made in many situations and contexts if writing is used to relate ideas and experience for different purposes. Deciding on the criteria for success which inform these judgements is a difficult and complex task. At all stages, pupils themselves can be actively involved in setting the standards for achievement, and as they become more competent so those standards, and their expectations, will be raised.

The Cox Report recommends that schools formulate marking guidelines, as one feature of a cross-curricular language policy. The intention is to establish:

- the purpose, style and tone of written comments;
- the basis for pointing out technical errors, and the manner of their correction;
- the techniques to encourage successful examples of language use;
- the part played by discussion with individual pupils in marking their work;
- the way marking will be used in connection with further learning, and hence as a crucial link in a coherent programme of study;
- the contribution of assessment to a pupil's record of achievement.

(Cox Report, 1988, p. 54, 10.46)

The writing curriculum, designed to support the child's development as a writer, also provides evidence of the child's achievements. Guidelines such as these could help teachers to be aware of the range of purposes for writing, and to plan tasks and give opportunities for an ever expanding variety of types of writing. Where possible, work will be related to topics, themes and issues on which the class are currenlty working, rather than random tasks plucked out of the air. This will involve not only a careful examination of the content of classroom writing, but also of its organisation and management, since this will reflect the teacher's attitudes to, and beliefs about writing. Sensitivity of response is as evident in the way that pupils are helped to prepare for writing, as it is in the encouragement given while engaged in the process, and in the comments made on completion. It is important to acknowledge that the relevance of the content is mediated through the pupils' knowledge and curiosity, and their commitment can only be secured where writing has significance for the teacher.

Positive messages are conveyed where;

- The teacher is not the only one to see writing. Children can discuss, share and enjoy each other's work.
- Children have time to write privately for themselves – diaries, messages, notes or journals. This writing is not 'assessed' but read and responded to if the child so wishes.
- Children are encouraged to type, print or tape record their words as an alternative to writing.
- All contributions are valued and children do not sense that they cannot write; tasks are matched to the children's abilities.
- There is no insistence that writing always goes into an exercise book.
- Time limits on writing are not imposed.
- Children have access to all kinds of books and print when writing.
- There is always a lot of talk and discussion about writing.

Some important considerations

Not all children necessarily appreciate the need for 'correctness', but writing has to make sense and it must be readable. Teachers therefore have to judge when and where it is appropriate to insist on legibility, accurate spelling and correct punctuation. Knowledge and understanding of the developmental stages in writing should inform those judgements. Some children absorb much of their knowledge of the conventions of writing from reading and it is gradually transferred to their writing. For others, the technical aspects of writing need to be systematically worked on, and the essential links between writing and the printed word fostered. It is largely in the development of technical competence that 'strategic' marking is necessary. It is strategic in the sense that it takes account of the child's capabilities, aims to boost confidence and is geared to improvement.

Essential features of marking are that:

It is done with the child, is positive and encouraging, designed to support and improve learning. It should not be anticipated as a form of criticism.

Children need to understand that work is marked in different ways, and for different purposes. They also need to understand the marking systems that are being used.

It does not attempt to cover too many features in one text. Sometimes attention may focus on qualitative elements – content, style, fluency or originality for example; at other times it might be specifically concerned with spelling or handwriting.

It has to be sensitive to individual needs, and take account of the pupil's abilities and understanding. It will therefore be selective.

The marking response operates while writing is in progress, so that errors and misunderstandings can be detected and help given. Waiting for work to be finished simply compounds the problem, and the opportunity for actual improvement is lost.

Whatever kind of marking response is adopted, it is nevertheless the case that a personal response is more immediately satisfying and can act as a spur to further thought and effort. E.g.

'I enjoyed reading this . . . .'
'What might have happened next . . . ?'.
'Tell me more about . . . .'

With younger pupils particularly, a verbal response is more appropriate than detailed marking.

Inevitably, the marking of written work has wider implications, not only in terms of time but also in relation to record-keeping. Increasingly, within the National Curriculum, it will be associated with assessment, with a subsequent impact on parents. Parents generally, are concerned about marking and where all errors are diligently corrected, take it as evidence of a teacher's commitment. It will be important, in the communication of assessment information in respect of writing, that success is measured by the extent to which it demonstrates the progress of an individual child.

The child's perspective

It may be that pupils are expected to do too much routine writing in the primary classroom, not all of which can be responded to effectively. There is a strong argument for reducing the quantity of writing that is undertaken when we consider children's own perceptions of writing, and the difficulties they encounter.

> The first thing I learnt to write was may name. I found forming my letters hard.

> I think I am often under pressure so you don't use your imagination.

Problems of finding something to write about, and new forms of expression are universal.

> I can remember when I was eight, that I wrote this story about someone called 'Wicked Witch Nella'. It went on for about ten and a bit pages. I kept on writing things like, so she picked up the flower, she put the flower in the sack. she picked up the sack, she put the sack over her shoulder. It went on like that for ages.

> I prefer to have my subject chosen for me. Otherwise I can't think of anything to write.

> Some kinds of writing are easy and I can write well. Sometimes I do not know what to write and it is boring.

The pressure of writing in a prescribed time, and of writing the required amount is keenly felt.

> My writing could often be much longer if we had more time. Once I took my writing out to play to try to finish it.

> When I was six we had a teacher and she always told me off for not writing enough.

The classroom itself is not perhaps the ideal setting;

> I am best at writing at bedtime when I'm used to reading

books. I once filled a notebook when I was six, I thought it was a work of art. It was the best work I did at that age. My latest story (The Search for Perfection) has, like all my long stories, been in my mind for more than a month. By the time I do get round to doing it, I have so many ideas I can't stop.

What these comments demonstrate, is that children know more about writing than they think they know. The difficulties lie in trying to find a form of expression for what is already in their minds. Our concern in the classroom, and therefore the responses we make, should be directed towards helping children to write what they really mean, rather than with trying to provide them with a formula for 'how to write.' We are reminded by Hughes that,

It is when we set out to find words for some seemingly quite simple experience that we begin to realise what a huge gap there is between our understanding of what happens around us and inside us, and the words we have at our command to say something about it.

(Hughes, 1967, p. 119)

CHAPTER 5

Evaluation and Assessment

The purposes of assessment

> Assessment is at the heart of the process of promoting children's learning.
>
> (T. G. A. T. paragraph 3)

Teachers have always been engaged in the diagnostic and formative assessment of pupils – it is central to their role. Nevertheless, within the framework of the National Curriculum, assessment will become more explicit and more extensive. It will be concerned not only with helping the individual child in learning, it will also be the tool by which teachers evaluate the curriculum in an attempt to secure progression and continuity in learning. In addition it will provide evidence of learning and support the recording of achievements and attainment. It will have an increasing impact on classroom management and organisation, and is likely to generate cross curricular developments and support differentiation in the curriculum. In embracing programmes of study, teachers' comments, observations and assessment will increasingly relate to statements of attainment, so that there will be greater comparability of assessment between teachers and between schools. The skills of teachers will therefore need to be more fully developed with regard to the formulation of activities, tasks and assignments with built in means of assessment, and in relation to the administration of assessment devices.

Language development and assessment

The Cox Report affirms the problems inherent in defining a linear sequence of language development. It is recognised that the assessment of language development must take account of and respond to, individual variation in progress and performance. The patterns of assessment proposed in the National Curriculum, draw directly on current classroom practice in curriculum planning and evaluation. Teachers, it is stated, have a 'view of the present achievements, pace and direction of desired developments for the class, within which variations can be devised for individual pupils.' This, it is argued, is consistent with a view of assessment as a way of 'taking stock' for,

> ...many children can reasonably be expected to know, understand and do certain key things in language by the end of the main educational stages of infant, junior, early and late secondary schooling, and that virtually all children, other than those with special learning difficulties, can be expected to attempt those things.
>
> (Cox Report, 1988, p. 30, 7.6)

The Report goes on to acknowledge the relationship that exists between assessment, curriculum and pedagogy, and recommends the principles that should govern assessment in English. It should be:

- a continuous process which reinforces teaching and learning, and not added on at intervals,
- an opportunity to check each pupil's performance by some form of structured assessment,
- carried out across a wide range of types of tasks, and in different contexts,
- an opportunity to assess the process as well as the product,
- a process, widely understood, trusted and accepted as clear and unambiguous in its operation and interpretation.

The relationship between teaching and learning is not always clearly understood, but if teachers are to devise an appropriate and effective programme of work, then they have to be aware of what children know, understand and can do. This information will be derived from a variety of sources including observation, discussion, pupils' own comments, tests and checklists. Where possible it will be supported by the actual evidence of learning.

Evidence of learning

Within a language development programme, writing provides immediate and easily retainable evidence of learning. If this is to be fully representative of a child's achievement, consideration will have to be given to the nature and range of the evidence, to the frequency and method of sampling, and to the part the child might play in the process. In terms of children's writing, the evidence will include rough drafts and finished products and the choice of items should not rest solely with the teacher. Gathering evidence will depend on observing children at work in different contexts so that writing products are sampled across the curriculum. Some written work will be considered in terms of specific assessment criteria, for example, Statements of Attainment; other work will be included as evidence of a significant and unexpected achievement. As part of the internal assessment of writing, it is recommended that teachers keep samples of writing as it develops over a period of time, building up a writing profile for each pupil. Children's own written work is the most reliable evidence of what they can and cannot achieve.

The writing profile

The writing profile not only provides the evidence on which judgements about progress and performance are made, thus serving a diagnostic purpose; it can also support the establishing of a school policy for responding to writing. This is particularly important in respect of issues of reliability and validity, and commonality of standards. Teachers will be making judgements about writing on the basis of their own observations, and through the use of Standard Assessment Tasks.

The implications of the context in which writing takes place also need to be considered. Moderation exercises will be essential and might include the setting of the same assignment to children of different ages. The results would then be analysed for evidence of growing competence, and the outcomes related to Statements of Attainment. Alternatively, samples of uncorrected writing products, from children of different ages can be collated, and used by a group of teachers as the basis of a 'marking' exercise. The procedure might generate questions such as:

- is the writing interesting to read?
- is there a logical sequence in the writing?

- is it original?
- is it lively and does it sparkle?
- does it contain complex sentences?
- does it contain grammatical miscues?
- is it properly punctuated?
- is there evidence of persistent spelling errors?

It is important in assessing writing that we allow for what the Cox Report terms, the 'gradual growth of sophistication, rather than just acquisition of additional skill'. This is more likely to occur where the scrutiny of writing samples is broadly-based, eliciting notes, comments and observations, which are then collectively examined.

There are long-term benefits for the pupil and the teacher in maintaining a writing profile, which will inevitably form the basis of a comprehensive language portfolio. It can be shared with the child so that the child is actively involved in the assessment process and has the evidence on which to begin to base decisions for improvement. An important feature of the writing profile, is that the child, as well as the teacher, is able to measure progress by looking at earlier samples of writing in the profile.

Studying a range of written products over time will enable teachers to more consciously 'notice' what children have written, and to be aware of the personal growth that is taking place – to see that what they write is an expression of what they are. The analysis of scripts is therefore an opportunity to look for strengths – to examine the child's success in reaching specific criteria, and also to pinpoint weaknesses and to plan a programme of support to meet individual needs. Shared with children, the writing profiles provide an opportunity to talk about general aspects of writing. To discuss, for instance, what is meant by story, poetry, fiction and non-fiction, characterisation and journalism, in order to establish the widest possible framework for the understanding of the forms and functions of writing.

Classroom observation

To complement the building up of the writing profile, teachers will be closely observing children as they write. Observation for assessment purposes means that the teacher is gathering information about the way in which the child copes with the demands of writing. Detailed observations might reveal some of the cognitive strategies being deployed, and so enable the teacher to respond immediately and directly to specific needs.

Observations of a general nature are being made all the time in the classroom, but working to the prescribed criteria contained within the Statements of Attainment will necessitate a more structured approach, and the careful construction of records. The systematic development and refinement of skills in classroom observation is therefore essential, so that teachers are not observing only aspects of behaviour. Observation has to be tightly-focused and analytical if it is to provide evidence of learning.

It is usually quite difficult to identify what is significant when observing children as they write, and records based on observations need to be related to the texts that are being produced. The annotation and interpretation of such evidence is necessarily problematic, but observation may generate knowledge about a child which is not easy to obtain or assess in other ways. On the basis of observation, it is possible at all ages and stages, to evaluate the way in which the child:

- is moving towards independence in writing,
- has achieved a measure of self-management when writing,
- enjoys writing,
- chooses to write when other forms of recording are available,
- is slowed up in writing by particular problems; spelling, orthography, access to vocabulary,
- collaborates with others (especially important with weaker writers),
- makes use of materials and resources,
- experiments with writing, trying out new forms of presentation, different structures, new vocabulary,
- finds writing tedious and demanding,
- approaches the learning and application of new skills.

Engaging in classroom observation enables the teacher to note opportunities for assessment, and indirectly, provides a good deal of the information on which curriculum planning is based. Attention to the context for writing can inform on the extent to which the circumstances are conducive to progress and improvement. It guards against making demands which are inappropriate or ill-matched to pupil ability. It serves to remind teachers that there should be every opportunity for pupils to demonstrate not only their present competence in writing, but also to be engaged in activities which will enhance their achievements.

Assessment lies at the heart of this (the learning) process.

It can provide a framework in which educational objectives may be set, and pupils' progress charted and expressed. It can yield a basis for planning the next educational steps in response to the child's needs.

(T. G. A. T. para 3)

It is intended that 'internal assessment for National Curriculum purposes should be carried out as an integral part of day-to-day classroom activities'. Because children engage in writing regularly, this poses few problems, and writing provides retainable evidence in the core and the foundation subjects. Time will also have to be found for observing the process of writing, within the wider context of general classroom observation. Before tasks and activities can be set, it will be essential to consider the kinds of information that are required as evidence of learning and achievement, and what has to be done in order to obtain this evidence. When allocating children to tasks, and in the choice of tasks, it will be vital to ensure that possibilities exist for differentiation in outcomes. This will involve careful lesson planning to be sure that there are arrangements for children at different levels of performance.

There are, therefore, significant implications for classroom organisation. It will have to allow for, and accommodate, systematic work with individuals and groups, on specific statements of attainment within the programmes of study. It is certain that as assessment becomes an integral part of teaching and learning, it will have a substantial impact on teaching styles and methodology, and on the management and organisation of the primary classroom.

CHAPTER 6

Summary and Conclusions

Many of the recent studies of the writing process, of writing performance and of writing development, have, predictably, introduced new areas for exploration. Wilkinson (1980) has emphasised that linguistic development is heavily dependent on the social and situational demands made on the learner, and not exclusively on an inner-driven, genetically-fixed process. Functional models such as Britton's (1975) describe development in cognitive terms, and link progress to an increasing ability to tackle an ever-wider range of writing tasks. Bereiter offers a provisional structural model in which stages are forms of organisation which may not be universal, nor have a necessary order. He refers to the relationship among his six stages as 'hierarchic skills integration'. In contrast, some critics of these studies, as for example Collins (1984), argue for a total rejection of the notion of stages of development.

What is increasingly obvious is that no single approach is sufficient in itself to account for how writing is learned, developed and employed. Cognitive development, as Donaldson (1978) has claimed, does not consist of the acquisition of new elementary logical operations. It consists, at least in part, of the acquisition of knowledge and control structures, that enable a child to employ cognitive capacities in flexible and deliberate ways on progressively more complex tasks. This would seem to parallel the process by which the child becomes a writer. Initially, writing grows out of a sound foundation of oral language, and, as the child matures, the structures used in writing, in turn, influence the development of speech. Later, there is a close and vital relationship between writing and reading which promotes the production of characteristically different linguistic structures. Drafting, revising, editing and planning all call for high levels of cognitive activity in their resolution and new strategies in ways of thinking are evolved.

Relatively little consideration has been given to the concepts of 'development' and 'maturity' in research into writing, or to education in general. Attempting to outline a developmental model which encompasses these concepts is necessarily an ambitious undertaking, and the model proposed does not claim to have done more than indicate possible directions. What it may have succeeded in doing, is to produce research tools (though not precision instruments) for the evaluation, assessment and analysis of children's writing, believing that to locate a script or text on a developmental model, establish its syntactic maturity, evaluate it according to judgement criteria and define its rhetorical purposes, is valuable. Syntactic analysis can provide insight into both the disposition of linguistic resources and their deployment.

It is inevitable that most linguistic and educational research in the field of writing development has its shortcomings. So much remains speculative and subjective even where clear guidelines and categories have been established. A good deal of information and description depends entirely on inferences.

At a simple level, the sentence is the largest unit dealt with, but writing is far more than the generation and accumulation of sentences. Problems within individual sentences are relatively trivial when compared with difficulties that arise in respect of the use of paragraphs, of thematic development, and of those other factors which contribute to what is called 'good writing'. Judgements about what is acceptable or 'mature' may have little to do with the function of writing. The Crediton Project (1980) for instance, in addressing the question of development in style, found that the criteria applied to discursive writing were not useful in dealing with 'creative' writing. Beyond a certain point, even length cannot be guaranteed to be a positive criterion – it can create confusion and hinder clarity of expression.

Equally, style cannot be described only in terms of syntax; we also have to appraise the integration of imaginative and poetic elements in the composition, and the effectiveness of a particular genre.

Carlin (1985), in a paper presented to the International Writing Convention at the University of East Anglia, draws some useful conclusions from his research into writing development in the primary school years. He notes that the theories about writing advanced by Moffett (1968), Britton (1975, 1977) and Bereiter (1980) all stress the close bond between writer and writing, and emphasise the direct link with cognitive maturation. In the current state of knowledge some generalisations about the characteristic features of stages of development in writing are possible. From basic narrative about a known 'story world', development is marked by the child's capacity to process in writing, increasingly abstract treatments of subject matter, and to write for a progressively more generalised and remote audience. But before all this is possible, as Carlin (1985) reminds us, the child has to secure the lower-order elements. He refers to children's own notions of the tasks – their difficulty in forming letters and therefore the need to concentrate on graphic skills and their careful deliberations in the crafting of a sentence.

If, as Bereiter anticipates, the child is able to successfully integrate the skill systems, cognitive maturation will enable attention to focus on:

- the process of getting ideas down (associative writing);
- shaping the associative writing in terms of style and mechanics (performative writing).
- shaping performative writing to have a deliberate effect on a reader (communicative writing).

As children exercise critical judgement and reflect on what to write and how to write it, other skill systems are deployed and further integrated.

Mechanical skills, Bereiter (1980) believes, can become fully automated without being completely mastered. Though it is far from certain that there is a universal sequence, children do share common concerns in confronting tasks and in making them automatic. (These concerns appear to have a chronological sequence, but this may be related as much to classroom practices as it is to cognition). Children themselves readily provide evidence of old skills being temporarily lost as new ones are being acquired, so that even while maintaining the general trend of development, there can be wide variation in products, and fluctuation in performance.

Although the foundations of basic writing competence appear to be laid down between the years seven to eleven, a surge of understanding of the forms and functions of writing seem to take place at about twelve years of age. This heralds a period of accelerated development in which writing becomes distinctly more personal and individual. The catalyst for this increase in momentum would appear to be a new comprehension of a reader, and although not all attempts are entirely successful, the differences in the quality of writing are too obvious to be ignored.

What also emerges from the Crediton Project (1980) and is supported by samples in Carlin's (1985) research, is that the writer's intentions, motivation and emotional involvement with the subject matter appear to be key factors in extending writing performance. In recognising the need for abstraction, in trying to be explicit, and in the conscious shaping of writing, the writer is making intellectual advances and cannot avoid being affected by the experience. What now seems to be important is to look at writing from the child's perspective, and to explore their attitudes and responses. An increase in the data collected on children themselves would be useful, of the type collated by Southgate (1981) in the research into children's views on reading. Earlier studies (Davies, 1973; Davis and Taft, 1976) of children's preferences for speaking or writing, indicate that there are some children whose preference for writing is predicated on a perception of it being a more private and personal mode of communication. This corresponds with Wilkinson's belief that writing is '...a prime means of developing the thinking, and the emotions, and of defining (and redefining) ourselves'. (Wilkinson, 1986, p. 8)

When children are emotionally involved in the undertaking, and writing about what is important to them, it is possible to work towards 'unique statements'. Writing provides a mirror on the child's linguistic, cognitive and emotional development. This is one of the chief reasons why the dimensions of writing are so difficult to define and categorize. Highlighting certain sequences, identifying skills and advancing theories can do no more than indicate general trends. Further research into the dimensions of writing development must, of necessity, as Beard exhorts,

> ...counteract the tendency of specialised linguistic research to neglect the personal construction of meaning and the associated affective and moral growth within the person.
>
> (Beard, 1984, p. 41)

What is evident, is that the complex nature of the factors which contribute to writing development, make assessment irrelevant unless it measures the child within the context of personal growth.

References

Beard, R. (1984) *Children's Writing in the Primary School*. London: Hodder and Stoughton

Bennett, N., Desforges, C., Cockburn, A. and Wilkinson, B. (1984) *The Quality of Pupil Learning Experiences*. London: Lawrence Erlbaum

Bereiter, C. (1980) 'Development in writing', in Gregg, L. W. and Steinberg, E. R. (eds.) *Cognitive Processes in Writing*. Hillsdale, New Jersey: Lawrence Erlbaum Associates

Bereiter, C. and Scardamalia, M. (1982) 'From conversation to composition: the role of instruction in a developmental process.' In Glaser, R. (ed.) *Advances in Instructional Psychology*, Vol. 2, London: Lawrence Erlbaum Associates

Boydell, D. (1978) *The Primary Teacher in Action*. London: Open Books

Britton, J. (1970) *Language and Learning*. London: Allen Lane

Britton, J. *et al*. (1975) *The Development of Writing Abilities (11–18)*. Basingstoke: Macmillan

Brown, M. and Precious, N. (1968) *The Integrated Day in the Primary School*. London: Ward Lock Educational

Brownjohn, S. (1982) *Word Games*. London: Hodder and Stoughton

Bruner, J. S. (1975) *Entry into Early Language: A Spiral Curriculum*. (Charles Gittens Memorial Lecture) Swansea

U. C. Burgess, C., Burgess, T., Cartland, L., Chambers, R., Hedgelands, J., Levine, N., Mole, J., Newsome, B., Smith, H. and Torbe, M. (1973) *Understanding Children Writing*. Harmondsworth: Penguin Books

Carlin, E. (1986) 'Writing Development – Theory and Practice'. In Wilkinson, A. (ed.) *The Writing of Writing*. Oxford; OUP

Clay, M. (1975) *What did I write?* Auckland: Heinemann Educational Books

Collins, J. L. (1984) 'The development of writing abilities during the school years.' In Pellegrini, A. D. and Yawkey, T. D. *The Development of Oral and Written Language in Social Contexts*. Advances in Discourse Processes Series, Vol. 13, Ablex Pub.

Davis, D. F. (1973) *Speaking and Writing: A study of socio-psychological correlates of skill in preference for the use of oral and written language*. Unpublished Ph.D thesis, Faculty of Education: Monash University

114

Davis, D. F. and Taft, R. (1976) 'A measure of preference for speaking rather than writing and its relationship to expressive language skills in adolescents'. *Language and Speech*, Vol.19, No.3

Department of Education and Science (1967) *Children and Their Primary Schools.* (The Plowden Report). London: HMSO

Department of Education and Science (1975) *A Language for Life* (The Bullock Report) London: HMSO

Department of Education and Science (1978) *Primary Education in England.* London:HMSO

Department of Education and Science (1982) *Education 5 to 9: An Illustrative Survey of 80 First Schools in England.* London: HMSO

Department of Education and Science (1984) *English from 5 to 16.* Curriculum Matters 1, An HMI series. London: HMSO

Department of Education and Science (1988) *English for ages 5 to 11.* (The Cox Report). London:HMSO

Department of Education and Science (1989) *English for ages 5 to 16.* London: HMSO

Department of Education and Science (1989) *Task Group on Assessment and Testing (TGAT). A Report.* London:HMSO

Donaldson, M. (1978) *Children's Minds.* London: Collins/Fontana

Duckworth, E. (1979) 'Either we're too early and they can't learn it, or we're too late and they know it already; The dilemma of "applying Piaget."' *Harvard Educational Review*, Vol. 49, No. 3, pp. 297–312

Dunsbee, T. and Ford, T. (1980) *Mark My Words.* (NATE). London: Ward Lock Educational

Emig, J. (1983) *The Web of Meaning: Essays on Writing, Teaching, Learning and Thinking.* Portsmouth, N. Hampshire: Boynton Cook

Ferreiro, (1978a) *The Relationship Between Oral and Written Language. The Children's Viewpoint.* New York: Ford Foundation

Ferreiro, (1978b) 'What is written in a written sentence: a developmental answer'. *Journal of Education*, 160 (4)

Galton, M., Simon, B. and Croll, P. (1980) *Inside the Primary Classroom.* London: Routledge and Kegan Paul

Gardner, W. K. (1981) *Testing Reading Ability.* University of Nottingham School of Education

Goodnow, J. J. (1977) *Children's Drawing.* London: Fontana/Open Books

Graves, D. (1975) 'An examination of the writing processes of seven-year-old children'. *Research in the Teaching of English*, 9, 227–241

Graves, D. (1983) *Writing: Teachers and Children at Work.* London: Heinemann

Hall, N. (1987) *The Emergence of Literacy.* London: Edward Arnold

Harpin, W. (1976) *The Second 'R': Writing Development in the Junior School.* London: Allen and Unwin

HMSO (1921) *The Teaching of English in England*

Hoey, M. P. (1979) *Signalling in Discourse.* Discourse Analysis Monographs, No. 6, University of Birmingham

Hughes, T. (1967) *Poetry in the Making.* London: Faber

Hunt, K. W. (1965) 'Grammatical structures written at three grade levels'. NCTE Research Report No.3, National Council of Teachers of English, Champaign: Illinois

Hutchcroft, D. M. R., Ball, I. G., Brown, M. G., Fairbairn, J. J. and Lavender, R. (1981) *Making Language Work*. London: McGraw-Hill

Kohlberg, L. (1963) 'The development of children's orientation towards a moral order: 1, Sequence in the development of moral thought'. *Vita Humana* 6

Kohlberg, L. (1964) 'The development of moral character and moral ideology'. In Hoffman, M. L. and Hoffman, L. W. *Review of Child Development Research*. Vol.1 New York

Kress, G. (1982) *Learning to Write*. London: Routledge and Kegan Paul

Kroll, B. M., Kroll, D. L. and Wells, C. G. (1980) 'Researching children's writing development': The Children Learning to Write Project. *Language for learning* 2, pp. 53–80. University of Bristol internal publication

Kroll, B. M. and Wells, C. G, (eds.) (1983) *Explorations in the Development of Writing*. London: John Wiley

La Brant (1933) 'A study of certain language developments in children'. Genetic Psychology Monographs, vol. 14

Marshall, S. (1974) *Creative Writing*. London: Macmillan

Martin, N., D'Arcy, P., Newton, B. and Parker, R. (1976) *Writing and Learning across the Curriculum 11–16*. London: Ward Lock Educational

Maybury, B. (1967) *Creative Writing for Juniors*. London: Batsford

Moffett, J. (1968) *Teaching the Universe of Discourse*. Boston: Houghton Mifflin

National Association for the Teaching of English (NATE) (1969) *Writing English in Education*

National Curriculum Council (1989) *About Writing Newsletter*, No 11 Autumn

Peel, M. (1967) *Seeing to the Heart*. London: Chatto and Windus

Perera, K. (1984) *Children's Writing and Reading*. London: Blackwell/Deutsch

Peters, M. L. (1967) *Spelling: Caught or Taught?* London: Routledge and Kegan Paul

Peters, M. L. (1970) *Success in Spelling*. Cambridge: Cambridge Institute of Education

Peters, M. L. (1975) *Diagnostic and Remedial Spelling Manual*. London: Macmillan

Peters, M. L. (1985) *Spelling: Caught or Taught? A New Look*. London: Routledge

Piaget, J. (1932) 'The moral judgement of the child'. 1950 Reprint of Ed. 1 1932, International Library of Philosophy, Psychology and Scientific Method

Raban, B. (1985) *Practical Ways to Teach Writing*. London: Ward Lock Educational

Rosen, C. and Rosen, H. (1973) *The Language of Primary School Children*. Harmondsworth: Penguin Books for Schools Council

116

Scardamalia, M. (1981) 'How children cope with the cognitive demands of writing'. In Frederickson, C.H. and Dominic, J.F. (eds.) *Writing: The Nature, Development and Teaching of Written Communication*. Vol.2. London: Lawrence Erlbaum Associates

Shaughnessy, M.P. (1977) *Errors and Expectations: A Guide for the Teacher of Basic Writing*. New York: Oxford University Press

Shipman, M. (1979) *In-School Evaluation*. London: Longman

Smith, F. (1982) *Writing and the Writer*. London: Heinemann

Smith, F. (1983) *Essays into Literacy*. London: Heinemann

Thornton, G. (1980) *Teaching Writing*. London: Edward Arnold

Tough, J. (1985) *Listening to Children Talking*. London: Ward Lock Educational

Vandell, S. (1987) Instructor's response guide to accompany 'Through the eyes of a Child'. Donna E. Norton. Ohio: The Merrill Publishing Co.

Vygotsky, L.S. (1962) *Thought and Language*. Cambridge, Mass.: MIT Press

Wells, C,G. (1981a) Language and Learning: Some findings and suggestions from the Bristol Study of Language and Development at home and school. University of Bristol

Wells, C,G. (1981b) *Learning through Interaction*. Cambridge: Cambridge University Press

Wells, C.G. and Gen Ling Chang (1986) 'From speech to writing: some evidence on the relationship between oracy and literacy.' In Wilkinson, A. (ed), *The Writing of Writing*. Oxford: Oxford University Press

Wilkinson, A., Barnsley, G., Hanna, P. and Swan, M. (1980) *Assessing Language Development*. Oxford: Oxford University Press

Wilkinson, A. (1986) *The Quality of Writing*. Milton Keynes: Open University Press

Willes, M. (1983) *Children into Pupils*. London: Routledge and Kegan Paul

Index